THE STORY OF EXPLORATION

EXPLORING
SPACE

ABDO
Publishing Company

THE STORY OF EXPLORATION

EXPLORING SPACE

BY ROBERT GRAYSON

CONTENT CONSULTANT
MARY KAY HEMENWAY
RESEARCH FELLOW
ASTRONOMY DEPARTMENT
UNIVERSITY OF TEXAS, AUSTIN

CREDITS

Published by ABDO Publishing Company, PO Box 398166, Minneapolis, MN 55439. Copyright © 2014 by Abdo Consulting Group, Inc. International copyrights reserved in all countries. No part of this book may be reproduced in any form without written permission from the publisher. The Essential Library™ is a trademark and logo of ABDO Publishing Company.

Printed in the United States of America,
North Mankato, Minnesota
102013
012014

Editor: Arnold Ringstad
Series Designer: Emily Love

Photo credits: NASA, cover, 2–3, 6–7, 8–9, 12, 15, 22, 25, 32–33, 43, 50 (left), 50 (right), 60–61, 63, 66–67, 71, 75, 76–77, 79, 82, 85, 88, 90–91, 92–93, 95, 97, 100–101, 103, 105, 106–107, 110 (left), 110 (right), 112–113, 114–115, 117, 120–121, 123, 128, 133 (top left), 133 (top right), 133 (bottom left), 133 (bottom right); Bettmann/Corbis, 16–17, 19, 30, 35, 44, 55, 57, 69; Nick Shanks, 38–39; fotosutra.com/Shutterstock Images, 38–39; Bob Gomel/Time & Life Images/Getty Images, 46–47; Dorling Kindersley, 53, 59, 132; AP Images, 89; Xinhua/Xinhua Photos/Corbis, 124

Library of Congress Control Number: 2013946596
Cataloging-in-Publication Data

Grayson, Robert, 1951-
 Exploring space / Robert Grayson.
   p. cm. -- (The story of exploration)
Includes bibliographical references and index.
ISBN 978-1-62403-253-0
1. Outer space--Juvenile literature. 2. Outer space--Discovery and exploration--Juvenile literature.   I. Title.
919.904--dc23

2013946596

CONTENTS

Outer space can be a remarkably cold, silent, empty place.

CHAPTER 1

SPACE-AGE WONDERS

Space is among the most dangerous and dramatic frontiers human beings have explored. Every mission into space begins with a bang, as huge rockets use controlled explosive power to leave the planet. Engineers and scientists must build these ships to precise measurements to keep this power under control. If things go wrong, a rocket can become nothing more than a gigantic bomb sitting on the launchpad—sometimes with people strapped on top of it.

But after the violence of a successful launch, the spacecraft silently drifts through space. Here, the beauty of space exploration becomes clear. The stars appear to shine far brighter than they do on Earth. The sun's light shines on the moon, illuminating craters and casting boulders' shadows across the lunar landscape. The colorful planets make their steady orbits around the sun. Far beyond the reach of today's rockets, galaxies and nebulas invite astronomers to explore their mysteries through telescopes.

The space between planets, moons, and stars is near-vacuum containing almost no matter. Because sound is simply vibrations traveling through matter, this means there is

A TOTAL VACUUM?

Although space is commonly referred to as a vacuum, it is technically not a total vacuum. Incredibly tiny amounts of matter still drift through space. Even in deep space, far from stars and planets, there can be several hydrogen atoms per cubic meter. However, this is so little matter that it has virtually no effect on human spacecraft. Outer space is the closest thing in nature to a true vacuum.

Many objects in deep space are so far away the only way to explore them is through a telescope.

no sound in space. However, this peacefulness does not mean space travel is safe or easy. On missions with people, spacecraft must protect their fragile crews from the harsh conditions of space. Life-support systems need to provide astronauts with air to breathe, water to drink, and food to eat. People must be kept at a comfortable temperature, and there needs to be a way to get them safely home again. If any of these systems fail, the lives of the astronauts can be in danger. These issues do not apply to robotic space explorers. But dangers still exist. In seconds, a simple engineering mistake can turn a multimillion dollar space probe that took years to build into a pile of wreckage on a planet's surface.

SCIENCE IN SPACE

Scientists and astronauts believe the benefits of space exploration greatly outweigh the potential risks. Space exploration, both piloted and robotic, has taught us incredible things about the universe we live in. This type of exploration is not the only way to uncover the secrets of space. Astronomers using telescopes on Earth's surface can also learn a great deal. For hundreds of years, this was the only way people could learn about the faraway reaches of outer space. But in the 1900s, technology began developing at an astounding pace. In 1903, the first airplane took flight. Forty years later, rockets were touching the edge of space. And in 1957, mankind's first satellite was launched into orbit. Now it was no longer necessary to investigate space from afar. It became possible to explore space from space itself.

With outer space unlocked as a new laboratory, scientists and engineers went to work building some of the most complex and

INTO ORBIT

Understanding orbits is key to understanding space exploration. Gravity, the force that pulls objects toward each other, is what makes orbits possible. Gravity constantly pulls Earth-orbiting satellites toward Earth. However, they are moving so quickly around the planet that Earth continually curves away beneath them, leaving them at the same height above its surface. Objects that orbit Earth are in a constant free fall. The satellites remain in space, circling the planet in the shape of an ellipse. Orbits must be above the atmosphere, the layer of air that surrounds the planet. If an orbit is too low, the satellite collides with air particles that slow it down. Eventually, it will slow down so much it crashes back to Earth. A high enough object can remain in orbit for thousands of years. Its altitude means there are almost no air particles to slow it down. Rockets give satellites and other spacecraft the altitude and speed they need to orbit Earth. They also slow down spacecraft so astronauts can return home from orbit.

Harrison Schmitt was the only trained scientist to walk on the moon. Most other astronauts were pilots.

powerful scientific tools ever built. Probes were sent out to the planets of our solar system. They returned not just valuable scientific data but also stunning photographs that captivated the public. The Hubble Space Telescope, a scientific instrument the size of a school bus, was launched into orbit around Earth in 1990. It allowed scientists to peer out into deep space in a way they never could before. Sometimes the scientists themselves participated in the exploration. In 1972, geologist Harrison Schmitt walked on the moon as a crew member of the Apollo 17 mission. He made key observations and selected important samples of moon rocks to bring back home for further study.

GOING TO SPACE

For people to explore space, engineers and scientists had to develop the space suits, robots, satellites, and space stations to make it all possible. In the process, they created materials and products people use every day and often take for granted. Many of today's innovative products have their roots in rocket science. Sneakers, tools, clothes, foods, braces, and eyeglasses have all been touched by space-related technology.

The National Aeronautics and Space Administration (NASA) leads US efforts in space. When the US government formed NASA in 1958, it wanted to be sure taxpayer money spent in space would also benefit people on Earth. Thousands of companies worked for NASA to build technologies and products for the space program. Many of them later turned those things into commercial products to improve people's lives.

NASA calls these products spin-offs because they apply the research done for space exploration to new and different applications. Thousands of them have made their way into people's homes in the last several decades. The tiny cameras in cell phones are one example of a spin-off. The technology to build miniature cameras used on NASA probes to snap photos of Mars and Venus came in handy for cameras in slimmed-down cell phones.

Sending people and robots into space also gives us a unique chance to look back at our home planet. Satellites with specialized sensors track weather patterns, pollution, and changes in Earth's surface caused by earthquakes and volcanoes. Imaging satellites give us aerial views of any place on Earth, accessible instantly through the Internet. Seeing Earth from outer space also reminds many of the fragility and beauty of our home planet. In a famous photo taken by the *Voyager 1* probe from the outer edges of the solar system, the Earth appears as a tiny blue speck within

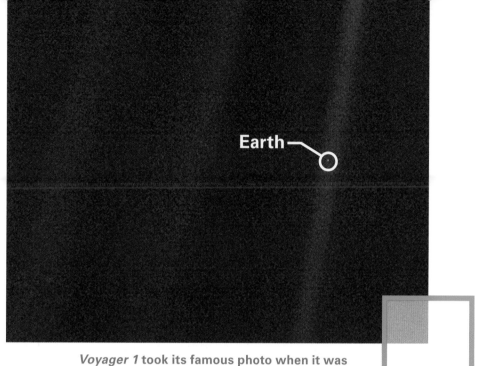

Earth

Voyager 1 took its famous photo when it was approximately 4 billion miles (6 billion km) away from Earth.

a huge void of space. In his book *Pale Blue Dot*, astronomer Carl Sagan reflected on the image:

> *From this distant vantage point, the Earth might not seem of any particular interest. But for us, it's different. Look again at that dot. That's here. That's home. That's us. On it everyone you love, everyone you know, everyone you ever heard of, every human being who ever was, lived out their lives.*[1]

The US military worried if the
Soviet Union could launch
Sputnik 1, right, into space,
it could also launch atomic
bombs at the United States.

CHAPTER 2

BLASTOFF!

A boldface headline blared across the front page of the *New York Times* on the morning of October 5, 1957: "SOVIET FIRES EARTH SATELLITE INTO SPACE."[1] The Soviet Union had launched the first artificial satellite in history, a shiny aluminum sphere called *Sputnik 1. Sputnik 1* was only two feet (0.6 m) in diameter, but observers in the United States could hear the radio beeps it broadcasted.[2] Americans wondered if the technology of the United States was falling behind that of the Soviet Union.

Ever since the end of World War II (1939–1945), there had been mounting tension between the United States and the Soviet Union. Though they had been allies in the war against Germany and Japan, the United States and the Soviet Union had different visions for the world once the war was over. The United States spoke in favor of democracy, while the Soviet Union supported communism. These competing systems of government led to a strained relationship between the two nations over the next several decades. The conflict became known as the Cold War. Though the nations never went to war with each other, they fought indirectly in many ways. One of the key battlegrounds was the space race, the competition to pioneer new achievements in space exploration.

The development of new and more powerful rockets was at the center of the space race. The same rockets that could propel a satellite into space could also carry a devastating nuclear weapon across continents. Showcasing achievements in space became a way to demonstrate military superiority. With *Sputnik 1*, the Soviet Union had taken the lead in the space race.

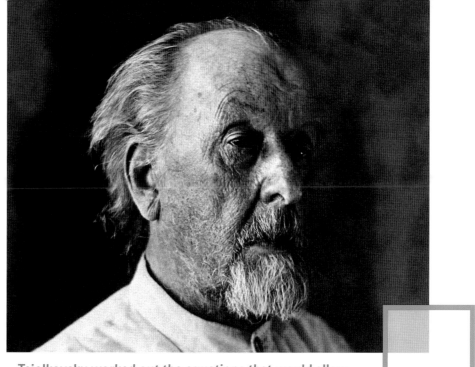

Tsiolkovsky worked out the equations that would allow later rocket engineers to leave Earth's atmosphere.

EARLY ROCKETRY PIONEERS

The launch of *Sputnik 1* represented humanity's first voyage into orbit, but the technological hurdles that had to be cleared before that point were immense. More than 50 years of calculations and experiments led up to the dawn of the space age. Three men, all born in the 1800s, played key roles in laying this groundwork. Russian mathematician Konstantin Tsiolkovsky, US inventor Robert Goddard, and

German physicist Hermann Oberth are considered the founding fathers of rocketry and space exploration.

In the late 1800s and early 1900s, Tsiolkovsky made the calculations necessary for rocket flight. He developed the basic theory of rocket propulsion, determined how fast a rocket would have to go to escape Earth's gravitational pull, and figured out how much fuel it would need to get to outer space. He was a firm believer that the best way to launch a spacecraft into outer space was to discard fuel tanks as they were used up. Getting rid of this extra weight would make it easier for the rocket to push itself upward as it traveled through the atmosphere. His work became the foundation of the Soviet Union's space program.

Goddard's rocket experiments in the early 1900s revolutionized

THE ROCKET EQUATION

Tsiolkovsky is well known for his rocket equation, which describes how rockets move using the relationships between a few key factors. The change of a rocket's velocity can be figured out if one knows the initial mass of the rocket, the final mass of the rocket, and how fast the exhaust is shot out of the rocket's end. The equation made it clear there were several ways to improve rocket performance. Rockets could be made larger, increasing initial mass. They could use multistage designs, decreasing their final mass. And special fuel could be used to create extremely high exhaust velocities.

the field of rocketry. He was among the first to favor liquid fuel for rockets. This kind of fuel would eventually make it possible to send people to the moon. Goddard proved liquid-fueled rockets would work by building and launching one from a field in Auburn, Massachusetts, in 1926. It flew for only three seconds, but it paved the way for huge advances in rocket technology.

Goddard then moved to Roswell, New Mexico, where he continued testing rockets and refining his thoughts on the subject. He developed and proved many theories about space travel in his lifetime, but they were not appreciated until long after his death. After he first proposed sending a rocket to the moon in his book *A Method of Reaching Extreme Altitudes*, the *New York Times* harshly criticized his ideas in a 1920 editorial. The editorial incorrectly claimed rockets would fail to work in a vacuum, since there was no matter to push against. The *Times* published a correction and apologized for the error almost 50 years later on July 17, 1969, the day after the launch of the Apollo 11 mission to the moon.

Goddard's first liquid-fueled rocket rose to an altitude of only approximately 40 feet (12 m).

Oberth was inspired as a young boy by the science-fiction writings of authors Jules Verne and H. G. Wells. As a young man he studied mathematics and physics at the University of Munich in Germany. He spent years researching gravitational pull and worked to understand how a rocket could escape Earth's gravity. Oberth realized a multistage rocket, which dropped used-up sections as it traveled in order to lower the rocket's weight, would make reaching orbit possible. He built and tested his own liquid-fueled rocket engines in the late 1920s, and he joined a group called the Spaceflight Society. Oberth taught a younger generation of engineers and scientists what he knew about rocketry. One of these students was Wernher von Braun.

WERNHER VON BRAUN

Von Braun would go on to become one of the world's foremost rocket scientists. In the 1960s, he helped design the Saturn V rocket that would take people to the moon. But in the 1940s, von Braun and Oberth put their talents to work for Nazi Germany during World War II. The war pitted the Allies, which included the United States, the Soviet Union, and the United Kingdom, against the Axis, which included Germany, Italy, and Japan. With the war going badly for

Germany, Nazi dictator Adolf Hitler poured money into the construction of *Wunderwaffe*, or "wonder weapons." These technologically advanced weapons would supposedly allow Germany to win the war. However, none of them proved decisive, if they worked at all.

Among the best known of the wonder weapons was the V-2 rocket, built by von Braun. The approximately 46-foot (14 m) liquid-fueled rocket carried an explosive warhead at its tip.[3] Technologically, it was a huge leap forward in rocketry. But it killed thousands in the United Kingdom, Belgium, and other areas. Thousands of V-2s were launched between September 1944 and March 1945. The attacks finally stopped when the launch sites were overrun by Allied ground troops.

As the war came to its end, the Soviet Union's army approached Peenemünde, the Nazi rocket research facility where von Braun worked. Worried about reports of Soviet mistreatment of prisoners, von Braun and his staff escaped

The United States carried out tests of captured V-2 rockets in the New Mexico desert.

the area and worked out an arrangement to surrender to US troops instead. Dozens of his fellow scientists and engineers surrendered with him and came to the United States under a secret US intelligence program called Operation Paperclip.

The United States wanted to get as much of Germany's scientific knowledge and rocket hardware as possible before the Soviet Union could acquire it. Oberth, who also came to the United States, worked with von Braun. Much of the German rocket technology and many of the scientists were already gone when the Soviet army reached key German military sites. But the Soviets still managed to salvage a great deal of information about German advances in rocket science. Both the United States and the Soviet Union began using German technology to kick-start their own rocket programs.

SCIENCE AT THE FOREFRONT

More than a decade after World War II, the United States and the Soviet Union began turning their rocket research into actual flights. By the 1950s, it was clear the two rival nations dominated world politics. The International Geophysical Year (IGY) seemed like the perfect opportunity for each to showcase advances in rocketry. The IGY was an 18-month project to gather new information on both Earth and space. Running between July 1, 1957, and December 31, 1958, it promoted international cooperation on scientific research. Both the United States and the Soviet Union worked to develop satellites and the rockets needed to launch them into space.

As *Sputnik 1* orbited the planet, people in the United States started questioning the nation's scientific know-how. Many wondered if US technology simply did not match up to that of the Soviets. The self-doubt would only get worse a month later with the launch of *Sputnik 2*. This spacecraft carried the first living thing to orbit around the Earth,

THE INTERNATIONAL GEOPHYSICAL YEAR

Sixty-seven countries took part in IGY activities. Findings and data were to be shared with scientists throughout the world. Among the areas studied were cosmic rays, solar activity, gravity, oceans, weather, earthquakes, and various other phenomena. The United States established panels of scientists to explore these subject areas, including one panel to study sending a satellite into orbit. The US Navy's Vanguard project was selected to accomplish this feat.

a dog named Laika. The Soviets were tracking the dog's life signs, including respiration and heart rate, in preparation for sending a human into space.

The space exploration efforts of the United States had been moving along without urgency until *Sputnik 1* was launched. President Dwight D. Eisenhower supported this approach. When the Soviets took a decisive lead in the space race, the American public pushed elected officials to pour more money into space exploration. US rocket engineers began working as quickly as they could. Thomas J. O'Malley, one of those engineers, remembered the general feeling following *Sputnik 1*: "We had one goal: to get something up there as soon as possible."[4]

MUTTNIK

Laika, the small dog aboard *Sputnik 2*, received a lot of publicity for her trip to outer space. The first animal to orbit the Earth, three-year-old Laika was a mixed-breed canine, prompting the American press to nickname her "Muttnik." The canine space traveler, who was part husky, was one of three dogs trained for the mission.

However, the Soviet engineers did not include any way for the dog to return home. Laika died from heat and panic just a few hours after launch. Modern observers have raised concerns about animal safety, but at the time many people simply saw the mission as another Soviet first. In 2008, a monument honoring Laika was unveiled in Moscow.

FIRST ATTEMPTS

On December 6, 1957, the United States prepared to take its first step into space. Without a unified space agency, different branches of the US military had been independently developing their own rockets. The US Navy's Vanguard rocket stood ready to hurl a US satellite into Earth's orbit on a brisk, sunny day at Cape Canaveral in Florida. With hundreds of reporters and spectators looking on, the command to fire the rocket was given at 11:45:59 a.m. As the ground shook, a ferocious roar could be heard as the rocket lifted off the launch pad. It traveled a few feet upward before falling back to Earth in a fiery cloud of smoke and producing a tremendous explosion. The launch failed.

With the pressure greater than ever for the United States to stake its claim in outer space, the nation turned to the US Army. The army had been developing its own booster rocket, the Juno I. Shortly after the failed Vanguard mission, the army attached the *Explorer 1* satellite to the top of a Juno I rocket and prepared for launch. On January 31, 1958, Americans held their collective breath

The explosion of the Vanguard rocket further shocked US citizens who believed their nation possessed the world's most advanced technology.

as the countdown reached zero. The rocket lifted off successfully, and *Explorer 1* was soon in orbit. The United States had its first success in space.

Six months later, on July 29, President Eisenhower signed into law the National Aeronautics and Space Act, which created the National Aeronautics and Space

Administration (NASA). The new agency began operation on October 1. By the end of the year, NASA announced a daring new initiative, Project Mercury, a program designed to send humans into space by 1961.

THE OLDEST SATELLITE

While the Vanguard program got off to a rocky start, it finally succeeded on March 17, 1958—its third try. The satellite launched that day, *Vanguard 1,* weighed only 3.25 pounds (1.47 kg).[5] *Sputnik 2* had weighed 1,120 pounds (508 kg).[6] The tiny satellite was launched into a high orbit, so few particles from the atmosphere slowed it down. It continues to orbit the Earth today and is expected to do so for approximately 1,000 years. Earlier satellites have long since reentered the Earth's atmosphere, making *Vanguard 1* the oldest artificial satellite. The Vanguard satellite program came to an end in 1959 with *Vanguard 3* as the US space exploration program moved on to the next generation of satellites.

NASA carried out exhaustive testing of the Mercury spacecraft before preparing to launch one with a pilot aboard.

CHAPTER 3

EARLY SPACE EXPLORERS

As the 1960s approached, space exploration became an obsession in the United States and the Soviet Union. Both countries focused on sending people into outer space. A major goal was to eventually land people on the moon. There was even talk of sending space travelers to Mars. But at the dawn of the decade, no human had ever traveled into space. Both the United States and the Soviet Union worked at breakneck speed to send the first man into orbit.

In the United States, NASA and its contractors busily worked on building and testing the Project Mercury spacecraft, which would one day carry an astronaut into orbit. The selection process to find astronauts was brutal. Candidates had to be up to the task both physically and mentally. They had to be experienced pilots with engineering degrees who had spent time in high-performance jet aircraft. Those who applied were subjected to a rigorous series of physical, mental, and psychological exams.

THE MERCURY SEVEN

When NASA first sent out a call for astronauts, 500 test pilots applied for the job.[1] The space agency whittled down the group to seven. Because of the cramped conditions in the space capsule, those applying for the job of astronaut could be no taller than 5 feet 11 inches (180 cm) and weigh no more than 180 pounds (82 kg). The seven men to become the first US astronauts were Alan Shepard, Virgil "Gus" Grissom, John Glenn, Scott Carpenter, Walter "Wally" Schirra, Gordon Cooper, and Donald "Deke" Slayton.

US OPENNESS AND SOVIET SECRECY

In April 1959, NASA held a press conference to reveal the seven astronauts of Project Mercury. They became instant heroes, not only in the United States but on the world stage as well. People wanted to know all they could about the men who had agreed to risk their lives in the name of US space exploration.

The seven Mercury astronauts knew one of them would be the first American in space.

While NASA dealt with an overwhelming number of media requests for interviews, the astronauts were undergoing training to prepare them for their upcoming missions. They practiced in flight simulators and learned how to control the spacecraft. They took part in experiments involving long-term isolation and followed extensive exercise regimens for building up cardiovascular and muscle strength.

Meanwhile, the Soviet Union assembled its Vostok spacecraft. Unlike the United States, much of what was going on in the Soviet space program was cloaked in secrecy, reflecting the general secrecy surrounding the Soviet Union at the time. Not much was known about the Soviet space program. Even the name of the person leading the space exploration effort was kept secret. The Soviet government would only refer to him as the Chief Designer. Even recruiting Soviet astronauts, known as cosmonauts, was cloaked in secrecy. The Soviet space program interviewed pilots at the nation's military bases with an eye toward recruiting them for

COSMONAUT SEARCH

With much less fanfare than in the United States, the Soviet Union started its search for candidates to go into outer space in the spring of 1959. Eventually, the Soviets put together a pool of 200 potential cosmonauts and began an elimination process. Some of the chosen 200 took themselves out of the running, succumbing to the strenuous mental and physical testing Soviet space officials put them through. Others simply did not make the grade, even though they completed the testing program. Finally, 20 candidates were chosen for the opportunity to become the Soviet Union's first person in space. The field would be narrowed to six before the Chief Designer picked the person to make the historic flight. The six finalists were the shortest men in the group of 20 potential Soviet space explorers.[2] In the end it came down to two men—Gherman Titov and Yuri Gagarin. Gagarin got the final nod.

space missions. But the fliers were not told why they were being questioned.

FIRST TO THE MOON

While the United States and the Soviet Union raced against each other to put the first person into outer space, both nations launched robotic spacecraft. On September 12, 1959, the Soviet Union grabbed headlines by launching *Luna 2*. The mission of the robotic space probe was to impact the moon. Approximately 30 hours after launch, *Luna 2* crashed onto the moon's surface as planned.[3] It was the first time something made by human beings had reached the moon, and it proved navigating a spacecraft to our nearest neighbor in the solar system was possible.

The Soviets had tried to land a probe on the moon before, sending *Luna 1* to the moon on January 2, 1959. *Luna 1* missed its target, but it became the first spacecraft to reach escape velocity, the speed at which it moves too fast for the Earth's gravitational pull to hold it in orbit. Soviet leaders celebrated the achievement.

KEEPING ASTRONAUTS ALIVE

Still, the top prize was sending a person into space. But this could not happen until scientists were confident a person could survive the harsh conditions of outer space. Researchers already knew outer space was cold and airless. They also knew that because orbiting is essentially a constant free fall, astronauts would be weightless in space. However, they were unsure how these factors would affect a person's ability to live, work, and think.

Additional danger came from the process of reentering Earth's atmosphere. When a spacecraft descends from orbit back to the planet's surface, it is traveling at an enormous speed. Once it gets low enough to start hitting the air molecules in the atmosphere, friction against the air heats up the spacecraft dramatically. Unless the spacecraft is properly shielded, the extreme heat of reentry

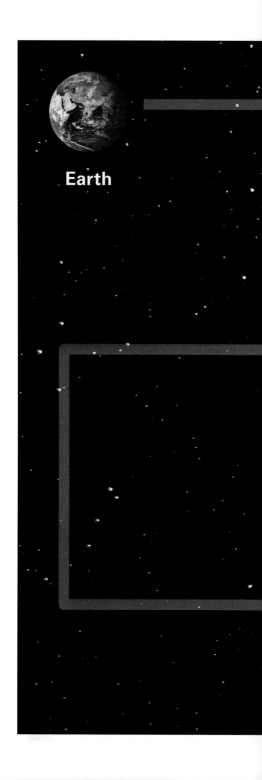

Earth

240,000 MILES (384,000 KM)

Moon

To-scale images give a true sense of the immense distance between Earth and the moon.

could easily kill a space traveler. Engineers and scientists worked to solve these problems.

US designers settled on a cone shape for space capsules, the sections of spacecraft where the astronauts sit. A heat shield on the wider end protected astronauts from the fiery reentry. Heat shields were made from ablative material, including special types of plastic or glass. Ablative shields are designed to burn away during reentry. Though this sounds dangerous, the ablative shield carried heat safely away from the capsule as parts burned away.

Space suits provided part of the answer to survival in space. Early models were simply modified versions of the suits worn by high-altitude jet pilots. Eventually, they developed into

ESCAPE VELOCITY

To exit Earth's orbit, a spacecraft must reach a speed of approximately 25,000 miles per hour (40,000 kmh).[4] Different planets have different escape velocities. The more mass a planet has, the stronger the pull of gravity it exerts. And the stronger the gravity is, the higher the escape velocity. The moon has only approximately 1.2 percent of the mass Earth does. Its escape velocity is approximately 5,200 miles per hour (8,400 kmh). One of Mars's moons, Deimos, is only a few miles across. With an escape velocity of approximately 12 miles per hour (20 kmh), you could easily throw a baseball into space from its surface.

equipment uniquely suited for living and working in space. These complex garments provide the wearer with an oxygen supply, communications, and controlled temperature and air pressure. While these suits might look cumbersome, they are designed to give space explorers as much mobility as possible while still keeping them safe. The helmet, made of durable plastic, protects a space explorer's head. A visor protects the astronauts' eyes from the sun's harmful rays.

ANIMALS IN SPACE

Before humans climbed aboard any of the early spacecraft, the United States and the Soviet Union used animal testing to ensure astronauts would be safe. The Soviet Union used stray dogs in the testing for its Vostok program. The Soviets reasoned that if stray dogs could live through the bitter winters in their country, they could survive the unforgiving conditions in outer space. In August 1960, Soviet dogs Belka and Strelka orbited Earth 17 times and returned safely. They were the first living beings to return from orbit alive.

The United States opted to use monkeys and chimpanzees in the Project Mercury test flights. NASA scientists chose primates because of how closely their genetic makeup resembles that of humans. A chimp named Ham made a suborbital flight for the Mercury program on January 31, 1961. Though he reached outer space, the capsule did not travel fast enough to enter orbit, and he returned to Earth in minutes. Nicknamed "AstroChimp" by the press, Ham splashed down safely in the Atlantic Ocean. Days before Ham made his trip into space, a new president had taken office in the United States. President John F. Kennedy was enthusiastic about space exploration and encouraged NASA in its efforts to send an American into space.

FIRST HUMANS IN SPACE

On April 12, 1961, the Soviet Union accomplished an incredible feat, launching *Vostok 1* into orbit with the first human space traveler, Yuri Gagarin. He orbited the Earth

The angle of reentry must be precisely calculated to avoid burning up in the atmosphere.

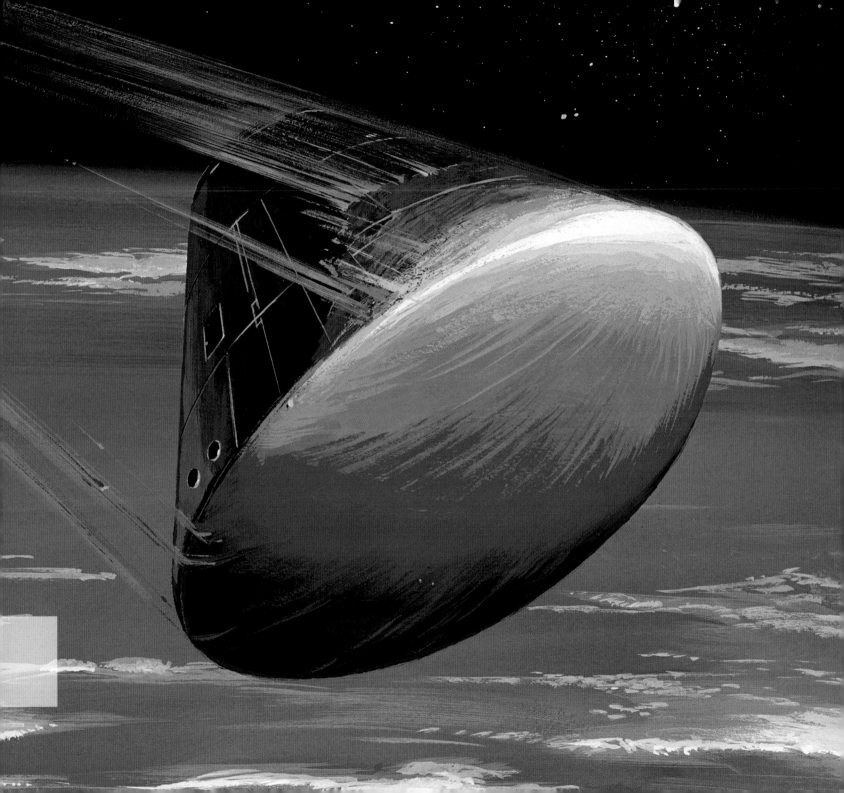

Gagarin's mission aboard *Vostok 1* would be his only spaceflight.

one time and returned safely. The trip took just 108 minutes from start to finish, but the Soviets could now claim a major victory in the space race.

Less than a month later, on May 5, the United States sent astronaut Alan Shepard into space aboard the Mercury capsule *Freedom 7.* Shepard only made a suborbital flight, reaching an altitude of 116.5 miles (187 km) during his 15-minute flight.[5] The Redstone rocket on which he launched was not powerful enough to propel his spacecraft all the way into orbit. "This is smoother than anything I ever expected," Shepard remembered thinking after takeoff.[6] The Americans had hoped to launch Shepard into space in March 1961, but an array of technical difficulties delayed the flight. Now both superpowers had put a person in space, but the race for leadership in the space age was just heating up.

Kennedy, *center*, made rocket and spacecraft development a major priority of his administration.

CHAPTER 4

A NATIONAL PRIORITY

Twenty days after Alan Shepard ventured into outer space, President Kennedy made a bold statement urging the United States to take the lead in space exploration: "I believe that this nation should commit itself to achieving the goal, before this decade is out, of landing a man on the Moon and returning him safely to the Earth."[1] At the time, the United States had a grand total of 15 minutes of experience with piloted spaceflight. A lunar mission would require a flight of at least a week. It would also require the largest rocket ever built, spacecraft capable of landing on the moon, and new technologies and materials not yet invented. Kennedy's challenge spurred NASA to develop the technology required to get to the moon. The Soviet Union responded to Kennedy's challenge as well, determined to put a Soviet flag on the moon before US astronauts could get there.

To land astronauts on the moon within President Kennedy's timetable, NASA had to quickly meet the key objective of Project Mercury: sending astronauts into orbit. Shepard's suborbital flight was only the first step. Following a second suborbital mission in July 1961, NASA launched the first orbital Mercury mission on February 20, 1962. Carried aloft

STANDING INVITATION

When President John F. Kennedy envisioned the United States landing a man on the moon by the end of the 1960s, he was not against the idea of cooperating with the Soviet Union. On several occasions, Kennedy tried to convince the Soviet leadership a joint effort between the two countries would be less expensive and might even lead to accomplishing the feat sooner. No response was received from the Soviets. Kennedy made one of these offers during a September 1963 speech in New York City:

In a field where the United States and the Soviet Union have a special capacity—in the field of space—there is room for new cooperation . . . I include among these possibilities a joint expedition to the Moon. . . . Why should the United States and the Soviet Union, in preparing for such expeditions, become involved in immense duplications of research, construction, and expenditure?[2]

by the powerful Atlas rocket, astronaut John Glenn planned to make seven orbits around the Earth aboard *Friendship 7*. But sensors began indicating *Friendship 7*'s heat shield was coming loose. That meant the spacecraft carrying Glenn could burn up upon reentry. *Friendship 7* was ordered to return to Earth after just three orbits.

Glenn modified his reentry procedure, but as he was coming back into Earth's atmosphere he saw a fireball fly past the capsule. If the burning object was *Friendship 7*'s heat shield, the flight was doomed. As it turned out, the ball of fire was only a piece of the ship that was supposed to drop off anyway. The heat shield did its job, and

THE ATLAS ROCKET

One key step in putting a man into orbit was building a rocket powerful enough. The Redstone rocket used for suborbital missions was not powerful enough to launch the Mercury capsule into orbit. The only rocket that could do the job was the Atlas, normally used to carry nuclear weapons. While the Atlas was effective when armed with a warhead, it crumbled under the weight of the Mercury spacecraft. NASA went to work replacing the rocket's thin stainless steel skin with a steel-belted outer surface. After a test launch of the redesigned Atlas rocket with a space capsule on its nose, NASA was convinced the rocket could put a Mercury spacecraft safely into orbit.

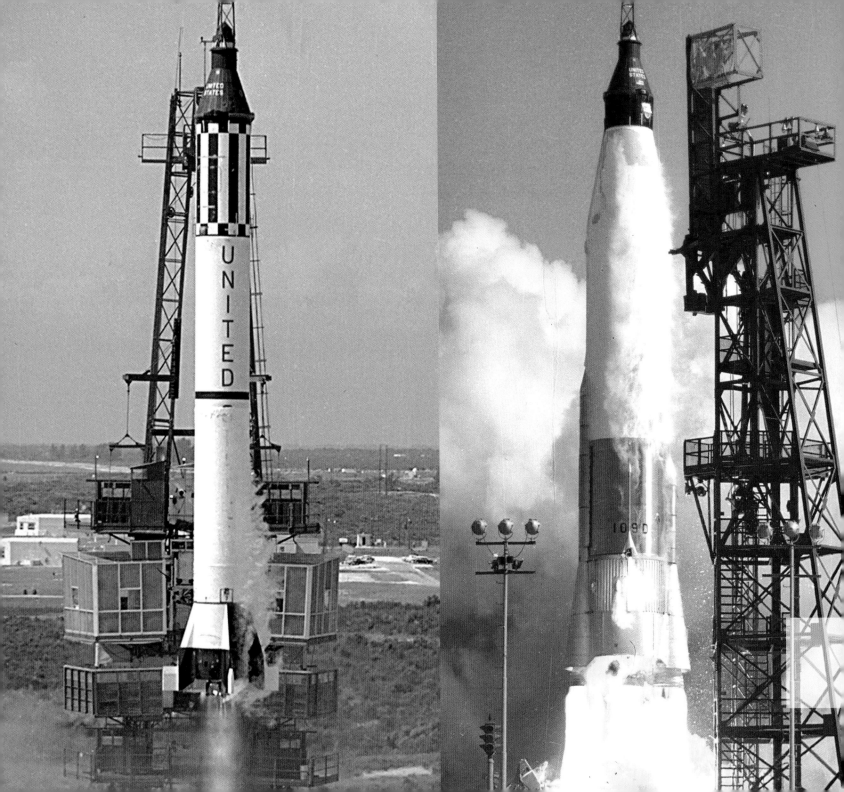

Glenn returned to Earth a hero. *Friendship 7*'s mission lasted nearly five hours.

THE SECOND GENERATION

Three more Mercury missions followed. The last one, on May 23, 1963, completed 22 orbits before returning home. By the time the Mercury program was winding down, the next generation of space exploration programs, Project Gemini and Project Apollo, were well underway.

During the Mercury program, the United States also pushed for breakthroughs in robotic missions. It had successfully launched the first space probe to another planet in August 1962. *Mariner 2* passed within 21,700 miles (35,000 km) of Venus.[3] Though it carried no camera, *Mariner 2* sent back valuable scientific data about the second planet from the sun.

By the end of 1963, the US space program was accelerating. But President Kennedy would not live to see

Early Mercury launches used Redstone rockets, *left*, but orbital missions required the extra power of Atlas boosters, *right*.

its next phase. He was assassinated in Dallas, Texas, on November 22, 1963. Vice President Lyndon Johnson, who succeeded Kennedy, carried on the fallen president's vision for the space program.

THE SOVIETS MAKE PROGRESS

The Soviet Vostok program had made five more trips into space following the success of Gagarin's flight. Two Vostok rockets were sent into orbit in August 1962—one on August 11 and one the next day. *Vostok 3* carried cosmonaut Andrian Nikolayev. *Vostok 4* carried Pavel Popovich. On Popovich's first orbit, he came within three miles (5 km) of Nikolayev.[4] However, the spacecraft were unable to get any closer to each other. The Vostok capsule lacked a powerful and precise reaction control system (RCS), a set of small thrusters that allows a spacecraft to maneuver while in space. The two cosmonauts were able to communicate with each other through the radio.

One of the goals of the mission was to study how different individuals adapted to space flight under similar

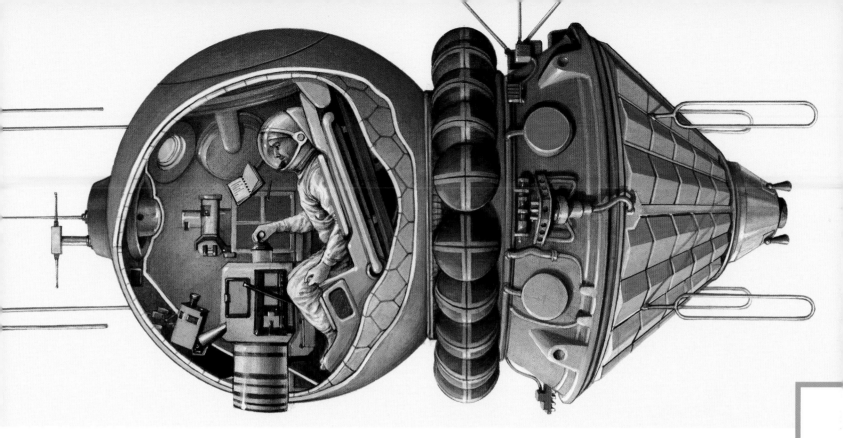

Vostok's lack of maneuverability meant it could not be steered to a precise reentry. However, its spherical design meant it could reenter without this precision.

conditions. Nikolayev and Popovich both returned to Earth on August 15. Launching two spacecraft into orbit only a day apart and bringing both back for a safe landing impressed scientists around the world.

Ten months later, in June 1963, the Soviet space program made history again with another double mission. Valery Bykovsky flew aboard *Vostok 5,* and *Vostok 6* carried Valentina Tereshkova, the first woman to fly in space. The Vostok program came to an end after Tereshkova's flight in 1963. Soyuz, the next-generation Soviet spacecraft, would not be ready until 1965. But the Soviet Union did not want to wait for the debut of Soyuz to launch a multipassenger spacecraft. They feared the United States would be first to send up a pair of astronauts in one spacecraft.

With that in mind, the Soviets modified the Vostok spacecraft so it could carry as many as three cosmonauts. The reconfigured Vostok was called Voskhod. Safety was sacrificed to make the change. To fit three cosmonauts aboard the first Voskhod flight, the men had to fly without space suits. As long as the spacecraft worked properly, the cosmonauts would survive. A trio of cosmonauts launched aboard *Voskhod 1* in October 1964. Wearing short-sleeved shirts and woolen pants, they completed their mission successfully and returned home. During the flight, the

EXPLORER IN FOCUS
VALENTINA TERESHKOVA

Valentina Tereshkova was working in a cotton mill in the western part of the Soviet Union when Yuri Gagarin orbited the Earth in April 1961. She was so inspired by Gagarin's mission that she wrote the Soviet government and asked to join the space program as a cosmonaut. Tereshkova was an avid and accomplished parachutist who worked hard to perfect her jumping technique. She felt this would help with her training for the space program. A few months after she sent her letter, the government responded by telling her to report to the cosmonaut training center in Moscow. By February 1962, Tereshkova was training for a mission. She was only 24 years old. It would be another 20 years before a woman from the United States, Sally Ride, would go into space.

Soviet Union had undergone a major political change. On October 14, Soviet leader Nikita Khrushchev was removed from office. Khrushchev had been a strong supporter of his nation's space program. It was unclear whether his successors would continue this support.

The next mission, *Voskhod 2*, was a two-man flight launched on March 18, 1965. It was a landmark mission for the Soviet Union. Cosmonaut Alexei Leonov amazed the world by exiting the spacecraft and floating outside for ten minutes in only his space suit. It was the first space walk in history. The United States had not scheduled a space walk until June 1965, three months after Leonov. It seemed as though the Soviet Union's progress in space was unstoppable.

Leonov's historic space walk represented yet another first for the Soviet Union.

MISSION IN FOCUS
THE TROUBLED MISSION OF *VOSKHOD 2*

Though *Voskhod 2* was a triumph for the Soviet Union, the mission was nearly a disaster. After Leonov's space walk, he had difficulty getting back into the spacecraft. His suit had stiffened from its internal air pressure, and he was unable to fit inside. He decided to carefully open his air valve to release some of his oxygen into space, allowing him to bend the suit's joints and get back into the spacecraft. Once he was back in the spacecraft, Leonov and crewmate Pavel Belyayev had trouble sealing the hatch. Then the automatic guidance system for reentry failed. The cosmonauts had to steer the ship into the atmosphere by hand using the spacecraft's RCS thrusters.

As reentry began, the landing module was supposed to detach from the orbital module, a part of the spacecraft which was simply supposed to burn up in the atmosphere. The orbital module held their air and water supplies. But it failed to detach, and the spacecraft started spinning uncontrollably. Finally, the landing module broke free and the spinning stopped. The landing parachute deployed, but the spacecraft was far off course. They landed in a remote area.

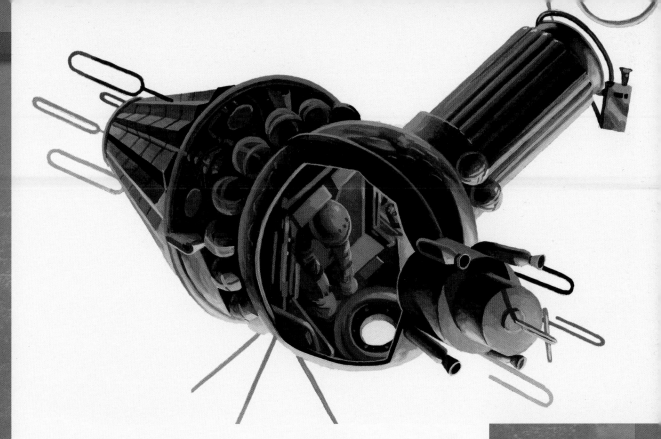

The cramped conditions inside the Voskhod capsule nearly cost the cosmonauts their lives.

Military helicopters finally found the spacecraft, but the area was so thickly forested they could not reach Leonov and Belyayev. The next day a rescue party arrived on skis. They brought food and water and helped the cosmonauts build a small cabin so they could rest before skiing roughly five and one-half miles (9 km) to a waiting helicopter.[5]

White's space walk began near Hawaii and ended over the Gulf of Mexico.

CHAPTER 5

TESTING LIMITS

June 3, 1965, was a beautiful day for a space walk. As *Gemini 4* started its third orbit around Earth, astronaut Edward White prepared to walk above the clouds. He opened the spacecraft's hatch and stepped out over the Pacific Ocean. Once outside *Gemini 4,* White remained connected to the spacecraft by a long hose providing him with oxygen and anchoring him to the ship. He floated gracefully at 17,500 miles (28,158 km) an hour.[1]

The first US spacewalker stayed outside his spacecraft a bit longer than planned. Mission Control had to repeatedly order him back into the spacecraft. White called the return to the spacecraft "the saddest moment of my life."[2] The American astronaut's walk in space gave him the record at the time. He walked in space several minutes longer than his Soviet counterpart Alexei Leonov had a few months earlier.

Working outside of the spacecraft was a key skill NASA astronauts would have to master. No one wanted to go to the moon without getting out and walking around. But space walks, referred to by NASA as extravehicular activities, proved to be exhausting and labor intensive. Even though astronauts were weightless in space, working in this environment was totally new to them. NASA would have to find a way to make the walks easier.

MANEUVERING THE SPACECRAFT

White's space walk came on the heels of the first piloted mission of the Gemini program, Gemini 3, in March 1965. The flight of Virgil "Gus" Grissom and John Young atop the Titan II rocket marked the first time two Americans flew together aboard the same spacecraft. It also tested Gemini's RCS. Sixteen small rocket engines arranged around

Gemini 3 was the first mission for John Young, *left*, and the second for Gus Grissom, *right*.

the outside of the spacecraft allowed the astronauts to maneuver in space. Being able to make fine adjustments to their position in space made it possible for astronauts to rendezvous with another ship in orbit.

Even with this capability built into the spacecraft, however, rendezvous remained a challenge. During Gemini 4, White's crewmate James McDivitt planned to attempt a rendezvous with an empty second stage of the Titan II. The stage had launched the spacecraft and followed it into space. But *Gemini 4* could not catch up with the target to complete the rendezvous. The spent stage was leaking fuel, causing it to move around. The Gemini spacecraft lacked a rendezvous radar, meaning the astronauts were forced to estimate the distance to the target. With *Gemini 4* unable to rendezvous and running low on fuel, Mission Control decided to abandon the rendezvous attempt and move on to White's space walk.

ENDURANCE IN SPACE

The problems with the rendezvous confounded NASA engineers,

CATCHING UP IN SPACE

Understanding orbital mechanics, the study of how objects behave in orbit, is key to achieving a successful rendezvous. One might think thrusting in the direction of the target would help you catch up. But completing a rendezvous in space can be counterintuitive. Increasing speed moves the spacecraft into a higher orbit, which actually slows it down. To catch up to the target, astronauts must fire their thrusters in the opposite direction. This drops the spacecraft into a lower orbit, speeding it up and letting it catch up with the target. Then a rendezvous can be made.

but they eventually figured out the complex science of rendezvous. In the meantime, the Gemini 5 mission focused on human endurance in space. Launched on August 21, 1965, with astronauts Charles Conrad and Gordon Cooper aboard, the mission set a new record by spending eight days in space. This eclipsed the Soviets' mark of five days in space.

Mission planners had determined a trip to the moon and back would take at least eight days. No one knew at that time if human beings could survive eight days in space and what the impact would be once they returned to Earth. Both Conrad and Cooper made it through the eight-day trip without a problem. However, having sat in their seats aboard the cramped spacecraft for eight days, they longed for showers upon their return.

MASTERING RENDEZVOUS

NASA applied the lessons learned from Gemini 4 when planning its next attempt at a rendezvous. Originally planned as another rendezvous attempt with an unpiloted target, the Gemini 6 mission was scrapped when the vehicle it planned to meet in space failed to reach orbit. Instead, NASA changed the mission plan and renamed it Gemini 6A. The astronauts would carry out the first close-up meeting between two piloted spacecraft.

Gemini 7 launched on December 4, 1965, and Gemini 6A followed it into orbit on December 15. Astronauts Schirra and Thomas Stafford successfully flew Gemini 6A to within one foot (0.3 m) of Gemini 7, piloted by Frank Borman and James Lovell.[3] NASA and its astronauts grew more and more confident about their ability to accurately maneuver in space.

A BIG BLOW TO THE SOVIETS' PROGRAM

Gemini 7 spent 14 days in space in December 1965. Despite the endurance record and other accomplishments of the Gemini program in 1965, there was no response from the Soviets. This was surprising, since the Soviet Union had taken

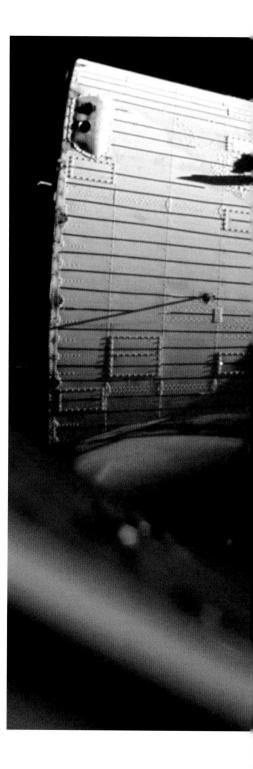

The meeting between *Gemini 7*, *far*, and *Gemini 6A*, *near*, proved precise orbital rendezvous maneuvers were possible.

so much pleasure in besting the United States in space accomplishments. Then, on January 14, 1966, word came that the Chief Designer, the leader of the Soviet space program, had died suddenly. The Soviets finally released the identity of their space program's mastermind.

The Chief Designer, Sergei Korolev, was a rocket engineer and spacecraft designer. He had been ill for much of 1965, but almost no one knew about his illness—even those within the Soviet space program had no idea he was so sick. Not even Korolev had known how sick he really was.

In December 1965, he went to the hospital suffering from intestinal bleeding. He was told a simple operation would take care of the problem, and he would make a full recovery. Korolev began bleeding further during the operation, and he died shortly after on January 14, 1966. After his death, the Soviet government felt the world should know who brought the nation its glory in space. Without the Chief Designer, the Soviet space program struggled to move forward. The Soviets would not schedule another piloted spaceflight until 1967.

Soviet officials claimed Korolev's identity was kept secret because they feared the nation's enemies would target him for assassination.

NASA PROCEEDS WITH GEMINI

NASA proceeded with its next launch, set for March 1966. *Gemini 8*, with Neil Armstrong and David Scott on board, had the task of completing the first docking of two spacecraft. Docking was the next key skill that had to be mastered for a successful moon mission. In docking, two spacecraft physically connect to each other after they rendezvous. This allows astronauts to easily pass between the two spacecraft. An unpiloted target spacecraft was launched into orbit approximately 101 minutes before *Gemini 8* on March 16.[4] Armstrong and Scott successfully docked with it. For 28 minutes, the two connected spacecraft flew together.

Then suddenly, without warning, the two spacecraft started to spin out of control. The astronauts suspected there was a problem with the target vehicle's thrusters. Armstrong undocked in an attempt to stop the spin, but *Gemini 8* began spinning faster. It was clear the problem was with the Gemini spacecraft itself. They later learned a short circuit had caused an RCS thruster to fire continuously. As they spun around at up to one revolution per second, the

Like all of the Mercury, Gemini, and Apollo missions, Gemini 8 ended with a splashdown in the ocean. Navy swimmers, helicopters, and ships recovered the astronauts.

astronauts were in danger of passing out. With no other choice, Armstrong shut down the main thrusters and fired *Gemini 8*'s reentry control thrusters. Finally, the spinning stopped. However, the astronauts had used up 75 percent of *Gemini 8*'s reentry thruster fuel.[5] Mission rules required them to return to Earth immediately, and the rest of the three-day mission was scrapped.

The next four Gemini missions refined rendezvous, docking, and spacewalking skills. Gemini 12, the program's final flight, featured all three tasks. The mission was launched in November 1966. Astronaut Edwin "Buzz" Aldrin walked outside the spacecraft for several hours. Before the flight he had studied ways to make space walks easier and more productive for the astronauts.

THE IMPORTANCE OF SPACE WALKS

With the Gemini program, NASA needed to perfect the art of spacewalking. Astronauts would be walking around outside the lunar module for long periods exploring the moon's surface. Space walks could also be lifesaving. If technical difficulties prevented the lunar module from docking with a command module after a moon mission was completed, the astronauts could make a space walk between the two spacecraft. Only the command module would allow them to return safely. The lunar module had no heat shield and could not reenter Earth's atmosphere.

HOW TO LAND ON THE MOON

The successes of Project Gemini gave the United States the unquestioned lead in the space race. Now the moon lay clearly in view. The method of getting there had been decided upon years earlier. In 1962, NASA planners chose the basic structure of the planned Project Apollo moon mission. A mastery of docking would be absolutely critical to its success. The mission structure was referred to as lunar orbit rendezvous. In this type of mission, one enormous rocket launches two separate spacecraft at once: the command service module (CSM) and the lunar module (LM). The CSM holds the astronauts, their supplies, and the engine that puts them into and back out of lunar orbit. It consists of the command module and the service module, which remain joined together for nearly the entire mission. The LM carries two astronauts down to a safe landing on the moon's surface. It is composed of the descent stage and the ascent stage.

The CSM and LM leave Earth's orbit together. After they reach lunar orbit, the LM separates and lands on the moon.

It fires the engine on its descent stage to slow down and come to a gentle landing. When the astronauts are ready to leave the surface, the top section of the LM, called the ascent stage, rockets into orbit, using the descent stage as a launchpad. The LM ascent stage meets up with the CSM in lunar orbit and the astronauts return to the CSM. The ascent stage is discarded, and the CSM's engine fires to push the astronauts out of lunar orbit and back home. At the end of the mission, the command module separates from the service module and returns to Earth. The astronauts' lives would depend on successful rendezvous and docking in lunar orbit. The lessons of Gemini made this ambitious mission possible.

The Apollo spacecraft was much larger than those used in the Mercury and Gemini programs.

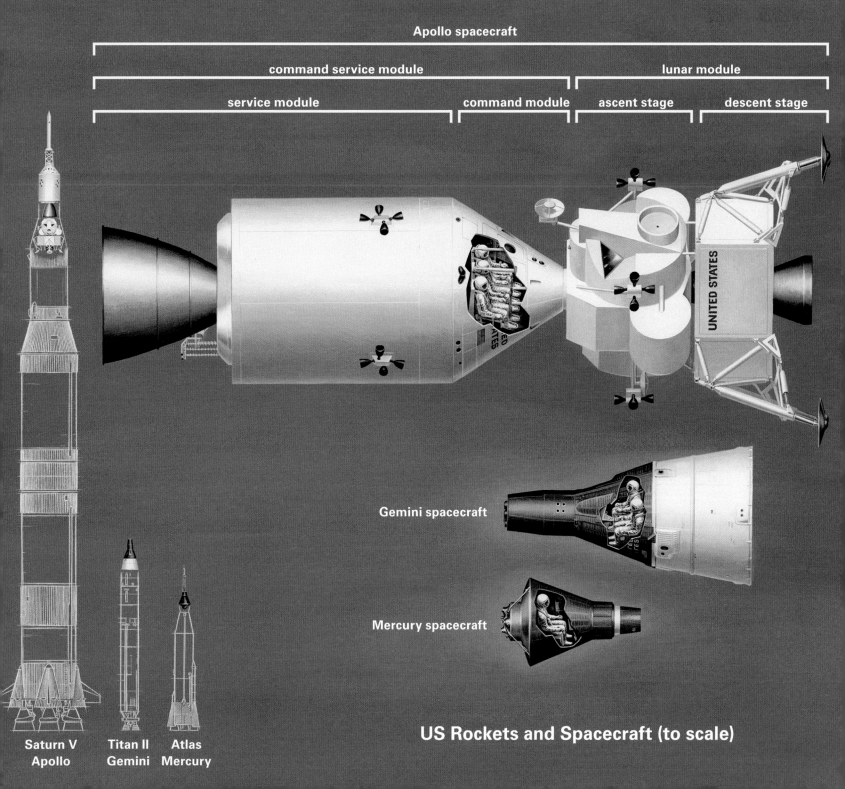

Apollo spacecraft

command service module

lunar module

service module

command module

ascent stage

descent stage

UNITED STATES

UNITED STATES

Gemini spacecraft

Mercury spacecraft

US Rockets and Spacecraft (to scale)

Saturn V
Apollo

Titan II
Gemini

Atlas
Mercury

Left to right: Grissom, White, and Chaffee were slated to test the CSM in orbit in early 1967.

CHAPTER 6

TO THE MOON

After the successful conclusion of the Gemini program, NASA was ready to move on to Project Apollo flights. Meanwhile, the Soviet space program, still reeling from the death of Korolev, spent early 1967 putting the finishing touches on its new Soyuz spacecraft. The Soviets planned to use Soyuz to travel to the moon. Following Korolev's death, his second in command, Vasily Mishin, took over. Many felt Korolev's successor was not as talented as Korolev had been. They worried Soviet progress would slow.

At NASA, the first piloted Apollo flight was planned for February 1967. The Apollo spacecraft would carry three astronauts. The first crew was made up of Grissom, a veteran of both Mercury and Gemini missions; White of Gemini 4 fame; and Roger Chaffee, on his first mission. The astronauts had concerns about the new spacecraft, the command module. But NASA forged ahead. A launchpad test was planned for January 27, 1967. The crew suited up and took their places in the command module, just as they would on the day of the real launch. The hatch was tightly secured.

For five hours the crew tested all systems and noted the faults they found, communicating the problems back to Mission Control. Then suddenly Grissom reported, "We've got a fire in the cockpit."[1] Flames engulfed the command module. The pure oxygen atmosphere turned the interior of the spacecraft into an inferno within seconds. Technicians working nearby ran to help the astronauts, but they were thrown back several feet as the pressure inside the command module blew the hatch out. Flames shot out of the cabin. When the technicians ran back with fire extinguishers, it was too late. All three astronauts were

The fire left the interior of the command module completely scorched.

dead. An investigation revealed more than 1,400 flaws in the Apollo command module.[2] With less than three years until Kennedy's deadline, NASA was forced to reevaluate the entire Apollo program.

SOVIETS ENCOUNTER PROBLEMS

That April, the Soviet Union planned to launch *Soyuz 1*, commanded by Vladimir Komarov. His mission would be ambitious, involving docking with *Soyuz 2*, which would follow him into orbit. Some in the Soviet space program, including Gagarin, believed the Soyuz spacecraft still had problems to work out before it could fly safely. Gagarin even demanded to take Komarov's place on the flight, knowing Soviet leaders would not risk the life of their hero in a faulty ship. But Komarov launched aboard *Soyuz 1* as scheduled.

Problems soon arose. First, a solar panel malfunctioned. Then other technical difficulties started cropping up. Komarov was ordered to abort the mission and return to Earth. The flight of *Soyuz 2*, planned for the next day, was canceled. *Soyuz 1* reentered the atmosphere successfully at first. But the main parachute failed to deploy. Komarov died when the spacecraft hit the ground at high speed and exploded. The *Soyuz 1* disaster severely disrupted the Soviet Union's space program. The next Soyuz mission would not lift off until October 1968.

The US space program got back on track after NASA redesigned the Apollo command module and finished work on the Saturn V rocket. In development since 1962 under the supervision of von Braun, the 363-foot (111 m) Saturn V rocket was the most powerful rocket ever flown.[3] A new style of testing was used that would put men on the moon sooner. Known as all-up testing, the system would test a complete Saturn V rather than test parts of it separately. On November 9, 1967, NASA launched an unpiloted command module atop the first Saturn V in the Apollo 4 mission. The test flight was a success and

THE SATURN V

The Saturn V was a prime example of the kind of multistage rocket envisioned by Tsiolkovsky and Oberth. Its first stage, called the S-IC, featured five powerful rocket engines, called F-1 engines. Each pushed the Saturn V upward with more than 1.5 million pounds of force (6.8 meganewtons). The stage burned approximately 200,000 gallons (770,000 L) of fuel in 150 seconds.[4] The S-IC's power output was roughly equal to the amount of electricity used at any given time by the entire United Kingdom. Once its fuel tank was empty, it detached and fell back to Earth.

The second stage, the S-II, fired its five engines, called J-2 engines, for a further 367 seconds. After it emptied and fell away, the S-IVB third stage burned its single J-2 engine to put the spacecraft into orbit. The S-IVB's engine shut down once it reached orbit, but the stage still had fuel left over. After the astronauts checked their spacecraft's systems, the S-IVB fired again to speed them up past escape velocity and to the moon.

Von Braun's crowning achievement was the staggeringly powerful Saturn V rocket.

after several more test flights, NASA was ready to launch the first piloted Apollo mission on October 11, 1968. The three-member crew of *Apollo 7* would test the redesigned command module.

PUTTING APOLLO THROUGH ITS PACES

The *Apollo 7* crew worked the command module hard, spending 11 days in orbit and testing every aspect of the spacecraft. That set the stage for the Apollo 8 mission on December 21, 1968. Astronauts Frank Borman, Jim Lovell, and William Anders flew the CSM to the moon and entered lunar orbit. Without an LM, they were unable to land. But the mission proved the United States had the expertise to reach the moon. Project Apollo was back on track.

Meanwhile, the Soviets were still trying to beat NASA to the moon. Problems with the planned Soviet moon rocket, the N-1, threw the program into disarray. The N-1 was to be even more powerful than the Saturn V. But its complexity proved too difficult to tame. While the Saturn V had five large rocket engines in its first stage, the N-1 included 30 small ones. An unpiloted test launch on February 21, 1969, ended in failure when the rocket exploded a short time after liftoff. The next launch ended Soviet hopes of a moon landing in the 1960s. On July 3, the next N-1 lifted a few hundred feet off the ground before falling back to Earth.

Packed with millions of pounds of fuel, the rocket blew up in the largest non-nuclear artificial explosion in history. The launchpad and surrounding facilities were totally destroyed. No one died, but the explosion left the Soviet moon program in ruins.

As Soviet engineers worked feverishly to correct N-1's flaws, the US space exploration program pushed ahead. Apollo 9 successfully tested the LM in March 1969, and Apollo 10 flew the combined CSM and LM to the moon in May. Apollo 10 was the final dress rehearsal before a landing attempt. The crew separated the CSM and LM, and two astronauts took the lander to an altitude of just a few miles above the lunar surface. Everything was now in place for the first landing on the moon.

MAKING HISTORY

On July 16, 1969, *Apollo 11*, carrying Neil Armstrong, Edwin "Buzz" Aldrin, and Michael Collins, began its journey to the region of the moon known as the Sea of Tranquility.

A total of 13 Saturn V rockets reached space; none of the four N-1 test launches were successful.

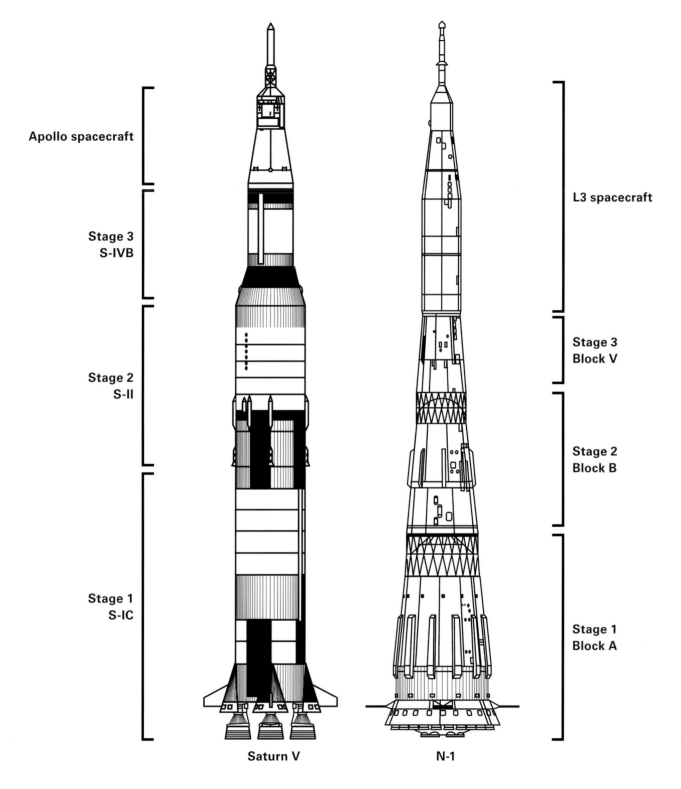

Apollo spacecraft

Stage 3
S-IVB

Stage 2
S-II

Stage 1
S-IC

L3 spacecraft

Stage 3
Block V

Stage 2
Block B

Stage 1
Block A

Saturn V

N-1

85

The astronauts entered the moon's orbit on July 20. In the meantime, the Soviet Union was attempting to achieve its own lunar first. Its robotic *Luna 15* probe was intended to land on the moon, collect a sample, and launch it back to Earth. The Soviet Union released the details of its flight plan to ensure it would not collide with *Apollo 11*.

In lunar orbit, Armstrong and Aldrin entered the LM, named *Eagle*, and undocked. Collins remained in lunar orbit aboard the command module, *Columbia*. Armstrong fired the *Eagle*'s RCS thrusters to back it away from *Columbia*. He then used the LM's descent engine to slow it down enough to land. Running low on fuel, Armstrong noticed large boulders in the planned landing area. He maneuvered to a clear area, touching down on the surface with just seconds of fuel remaining. He landed it so gently

THE MOON'S SEAS

Astronomers who looked up at the moon saw some areas that seemed darker than others. They called them seas. Besides the Sea of Tranquility, there are the Sea of Fertility, the Sea of Nectar, the Sea of Crises, and the Ocean of Storms. Though they are called seas, they contain no water. The dark areas were formed by volcanic eruptions. They have fewer craters than the rest of the lunar surface, making them smoother and more attractive landing sites.

there was little impact. Armstrong proclaimed, "Houston, Tranquility Base here. The Eagle has landed."[5]

Armstrong was the first to exit the LM and walk on the moon. As he set foot on the lunar surface, he said, "That's one small step for a man; one giant leap for mankind."[6] Aldrin soon followed him. The pair hopped along carefully in the moon's low gravity, one-sixth that on Earth. They conducted experiments and collected rocks and soil samples to bring home. After a moon walk that lasted approximately two and one-half hours, the astronauts got back into the *Eagle*. They slept, then prepared to return to Earth. They fired the ascent engine, separating the two halves of the *Eagle* and launching themselves back into lunar orbit. Using the techniques worked out on the previous Gemini and Apollo missions, they docked with *Columbia*. Armstrong and Aldrin joined Collins in *Columbia*, fired the CSM's engine, and blasted out of lunar orbit toward Earth. They splashed down safely in the Pacific Ocean on July 24.

EXPLORER IN FOCUS
NEIL ARMSTRONG

Neil Armstrong was born in Wapakoneta, Ohio, in 1930. He was a US Navy fighter pilot during the Korean War (1950–1953). During one mission, enemy fire hit his plane, damaging the right wing. Still, he skillfully guided it back to friendly territory.

Armstrong received a bachelor's degree in aeronautical engineering from Purdue University in 1955. The same year, he became a civilian test pilot for NACA, the forerunner to NASA. He flew more than 200 different types of aircraft.[7] Armstrong was chosen for the space program in 1962 as part of NASA's New Nine, the next group of astronauts selected after the Mercury Seven.

Armstrong's first steps on the moon were broadcast around the world in a grainy television image.

The United States had landed astronauts on the moon and returned them home. Hours after Armstrong and Aldrin set foot on the lunar surface, *Luna 15* crashed into a mountain on the moon and lost contact with Earth. It was clear the United States had decisively won the space race.

Apollo 15 astronaut Jim Irwin saluted the US flag on the lunar surface beside the LM *Falcon* and the lunar roving vehicle.

CHAPTER 7

AFTER THE RACE

Though the United States won the race to the moon, space exploration did not stop with Apollo 11. Six more US missions flew to the moon between November 1969 and December 1972. Apollo 13 nearly ended in disaster when an explosion crippled the service module. Improvisation on the part of the crew and ground controllers led to the use of the LM as a lifeboat, allowing the astronauts to survive for several days until gravity brought them home again. Altogether, 12 astronauts walked on the lunar surface during the Apollo program. Mission durations increased as NASA gained more experience working on the moon. Apollo 15,

Apollo 16, and Apollo 17 were three-day stays on the moon. They involved multiple moonwalks, more science experiments, and the use of the lunar roving vehicle to explore more of the moon's surface.

LUNAR ROVING

Starting with Apollo 15, getting around on the moon got a lot easier. For the first time, the astronauts brought along their own car. The lunar roving vehicle, approximately ten feet (3 m) long and four feet (1.2 m) high, resembled a small car. It allowed the astronauts to travel farther than they ever had on the moon's surface. Traveling along at eight miles per hour (13 kmh), the rover was equipped with a television camera and computer.[1] The battery-powered rover arrived on the moon folded up and attached to the inside of the lunar module. Astronauts unloaded and unfolded the vehicle. Three lunar roving vehicles remain on the Moon's surface today, parked in their final resting places.

Leftover hardware was used in two new missions in the 1970s. The first was Skylab, the first US space station. Three crews visited the station in 1973 and 1974. In the 1975 Apollo-Soyuz Test Project, an Apollo command module docked with a Soyuz spacecraft in orbit around Earth. The crews shook hands and exchanged gifts.

APOLLO TELESCOPE MOUNT

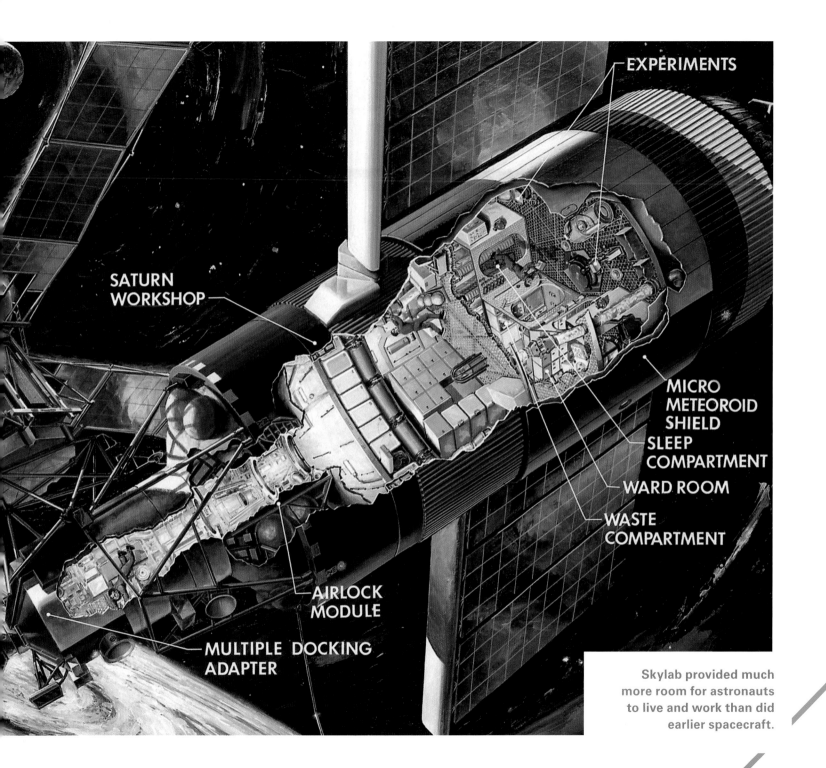

EXPERIMENTS

SATURN
WORKSHOP

MICRO
METEOROID
SHIELD
SLEEP
COMPARTMENT

WARD ROOM

WASTE
COMPARTMENT

AIRLOCK
MODULE

MULTIPLE DOCKING
ADAPTER

Skylab provided much
more room for astronauts
to live and work than did
earlier spacecraft.

MISSION IN FOCUS
APOLLO-SOYUZ TEST PROJECT

International cooperation in space started out with an exchange of letters. NASA administrator Thomas O. Paine and Mstislav Keldysh, president of the Soviet Academy of Sciences, began corresponding just after Apollo 11. The two scientists believed their nations could work together on a joint space venture. By October 1970, representatives of both countries were meeting to work out the details of the Apollo-Soyuz Test Project (ASTP).

One of the major accomplishments of the mission happened before it even left the ground. The two nations shared detailed information about their space programs in order to make the ASTP successful. Three NASA astronauts assigned to the mission were allowed to inspect the Soyuz spacecraft and launchpad early in the flight planning stages, an unprecedented move for the Soviet Union.

The spacecraft were launched from their respective nations on July 15, 1975. The Apollo command module, with Thomas Stafford, Donald "Deke" Slayton, and Vance Brand aboard, docked with the Soyuz space capsule carrying Alexei Leonov and Valeri Kubasov on July 17. The international cooperation exhibited by the ASTP eventually culminated in the International Space Station.

The flight was part of a wider attempt to defuse tensions between the United States and the Soviet Union.

With the close of the Apollo era, NASA turned its attention to designing a reusable space vehicle. The space agency wanted to build a spacecraft that could be launched like a rocket and return to Earth like an airplane. NASA officially called this bold project the Space Transportation System (STS). It became best known as the space shuttle. The reusable ship was viewed as a more economical way to explore space. The spacecraft used in the Mercury, Gemini, and Apollo programs were so thoroughly damaged during reentry they could only be used one time. NASA hoped the shuttle would make space travel a routine event. Planners hoped for shuttle missions to begin as early as 1977, but design problems and other delays kept the STS out of space until 1981.

FAR-REACHING PROBES

While NASA developed the space shuttle, the United States embarked on a series of successful and far-reaching robotic

Pioneer 10 continued to transmit data to Earth until 2003, when communication ended due to a loss of power.

missions. *Pioneer 10* was launched on March 2, 1972. Twenty months later, it became the first probe to approach Jupiter, the solar system's largest planet. Without a powerful engine to slow it down into Jupiter's orbit, *Pioneer 10* was only able to observe the planet as it flew past it. But the probe got close enough to take photos of the gas-covered planet's powerful storms. *Pioneer 11*, launched on April 5, 1973, flew to Jupiter and also observed Saturn.

Between the 1960s and the 1980s, the Soviet Union took the lead in exploring Venus, the second planet from the sun. The planet's high pressure and temperature make it a difficult place to explore. Still, the Soviet Union successfully landed several of its Venera probes on the surface. *Venera 7*, landing on December 15, 1970, was the first spacecraft to land on another planet. It functioned for less than an hour after landing, but it sent back valuable data.

Both the Soviet Union and the United States sent probes to Mars in the 1960s and 1970s. NASA's *Mariner 4* was the first spacecraft to reach the planet, doing so in 1965. The Soviet Union's *Mars 3* was the first to successfully land on its surface, though its communications with Earth failed only 20 seconds after landing. NASA's first Mars landers, *Viking 1* and *Viking 2*, were launched in August and September 1975.[2] Both landed successfully. Together, they sent back hundreds of images from the surface.

AN INHOSPITABLE PLANET

Venus is among the hardest places in the solar system to explore. The planet is only slightly smaller than Earth, but it differs significantly in the conditions at its surface. The temperature averages 867 degrees Fahrenheit (464°C), and the air pressure is a crushing 90 times higher than on Earth.[3] The atmosphere is nearly entirely carbon dioxide, and acid rains from the sky. None of the Venera probes lasted even three hours on the surface before being destroyed by the harsh conditions.

In the 1960s, astronomers realized an incredible chance to study the outer solar system was on the horizon. In the late 1970s, Jupiter, Saturn, Uranus, and Neptune would align in a way that would make it possible to visit them all in a single mission. NASA developed the Voyager program to take advantage of this opportunity. *Voyager 2* was launched in August 1977, and *Voyager 1* was launched in September. *Voyager 2* went on what was known as a "grand tour." It flew past Jupiter (July 1979), Saturn (August 1981), Uranus (January 1986), and Neptune (August 1989). *Voyager 1* visited just Jupiter and Saturn. Both *Voyager 2* and *Voyager 1* are still functional and communicating with Earth. They continue studying the far edge of the solar system beyond the planets.

CUTTING-EDGE SPACE PLANE

When the space shuttle was finally completed, it was hailed by NASA as the future of spaceflight. Its first mission, STS-1, was launched on April 12, 1981, with astronauts John Young and Robert Crippen aboard *Columbia*. Young and Crippen were the first Americans to go into space since the Apollo-Soyuz Test Project in 1975.

Three major components made up the space shuttle at launch—the orbiter, an external fuel tank, and solid rocket boosters (SRBs). The orbiter holds the astronauts; it is the only part that reaches orbit. The external fuel tank holds liquid fuel for the three space shuttle main engines (SSMEs), located at the back of the orbiter. Once it is empty, the tank drops away and falls back to Earth. The external tank is not reused. The SRBs give the shuttle extra thrust for liftoff. Rather than the liquid fuels used by F-1 engines, J-2 engines, and SSMEs, the SRBs use a solid fuel. Once they run out of this fuel, the SRBs fall off and parachute into the ocean. They are then recovered and reused. When the shuttle returns to Earth, it uses its wings to glide to a landing on a runway.

Space shuttles have been used to deploy satellites, repair existing satellites, and conduct

Each SRB produced nearly
twice the thrust of the
Saturn V's F-1 engine.

science experiments. A space shuttle put the Hubble Space Telescope (HST) into orbit in 1990. The 24,500-pound (11,113 kg) telescope measures 43.5 feet (13.3 m) across.[4] It still functions today. The HST has provided scientists with extremely sharp images of stars, galaxies, and more. The telescope has had a major impact on astronomical research, supplying data that would otherwise have been unattainable. When it was first launched, scientists discovered with dismay that its primary mirror, critical for making sharp images, was flawed. A repair mission launched in 1993 brought astronauts back to the HST to make adjustments. The extremely complex mission involved multiple space walks. It was a success, and sharp images soon began coming from the HST.

SHUTTLE DISASTERS

While the space shuttle program racked up numerous accomplishments, it also suffered two major disasters that cost the lives of 14 astronauts. The *Challenger,* one of four US space shuttles, had made nine flights by the end of 1985. Its next mission, on January 28, 1986, was special because

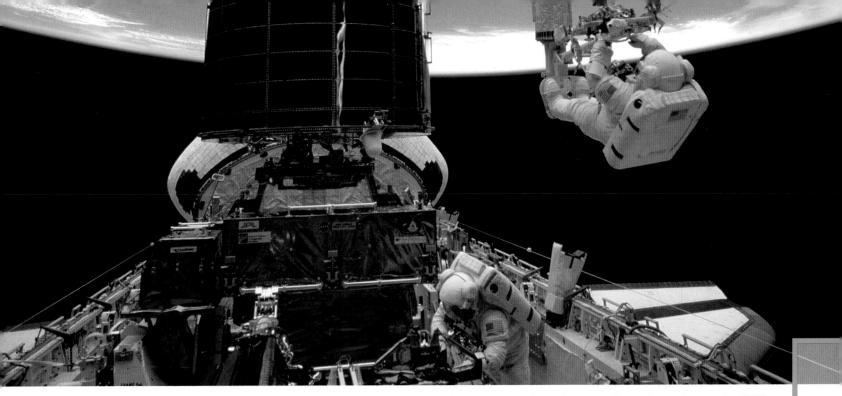

Astronauts worked in shifts of two to complete the complicated repairs on the HST.

one of the crew members going into space was not a professional astronaut. She was a high school social studies teacher. Christa McAuliffe of Concord, New Hampshire, was scheduled to conduct experiments aboard the *Challenger* and teach two classes from outer space. She and six other crew members—Ellison Onizuka, Gregory Jarvis, Judith Resnick, Michael Smith, Francis Scobee, and Ronald McNair—died when the *Challenger* exploded just 73 seconds after liftoff.[5] A failure in one of the SRBs was found to be responsible for the disaster. The first post-*Challenger* mission came on September 29, 1988, when the space shuttle *Discovery* was launched.

Another disaster struck on February 1, 2003. The space shuttle *Columbia* disintegrated while reentering the atmosphere. Rick Husband, Ilan Ramon, Laurel Clark, Michael Anderson, William McCool, David Brown, and Kalpana Chawla all died in the accident. An investigation determined damage to the spacecraft during liftoff caused the accident. A piece of insulating foam from the external fuel tank broke away and punctured the heat shield on the edge of the left wing. When the shuttle reentered, hot gases created by friction against the atmosphere got into the wing, destroying the vehicle.

The *Columbia* disaster kept the remaining shuttle fleet out

THE FLEET

NASA originally built four shuttles for space missions: *Columbia*, *Challenger*, *Discovery*, and *Atlantis*. Another, *Enterprise*, was built only for test flights in the atmosphere. It was unable to go into space. After *Challenger* was destroyed, NASA built a new shuttle, *Endeavour*. No replacement was built for *Columbia*. Today, the surviving shuttles can be seen in museums across the United States.

NASA brought all debris from the *Columbia* disaster to a warehouse for analysis.

of the sky for two and a half years. When flights started up again in July 2005, the shuttle fleet completed the rest of its missions without incident. The shuttle's last mission, STS-135, came on July 8, 2011, after which the program came to a close, and the spacecraft was retired. In total, 135 missions were flown.[6] The United States has not put its own piloted spacecraft into space since the last shuttle mission.

Mir represented the culmination of Soviet space station technology.

CHAPTER 8

ORBITING SCIENCE LABS

In the 1970s and 1980s, the Soviet Union took the lead in developing space station technology. It launched the first space station, Salyut 1, in April 1971, and the crew of Soyuz 11 boarded it in June. The success of the space station was overshadowed by the deaths of the Soyuz 11 crew upon their reentry. A valve to space accidentally opened, and the crew's air blew out into space, suffocating them. Still, the spacecraft reentered normally. Recovery crews were the first to discover the death of the cosmonauts when they opened the hatch.

After the tragedy, the Soviet Union continued to commit itself to a robust space station program. The Mir space station, the largest to that point, orbited Earth between 1986 and 2001. Astronauts and cosmonauts from several nations worked aboard Mir during its lifetime, including many who arrived in docked US space shuttles.

SUPERPOWER TEAMWORK

Once the Soviet Union disbanded in 1991, a new spirit of space cooperation developed between Russia and the United States. The Russian Federal Space Agency expressed interest when NASA suggested Russia join a new space station project. In September 1993, Russia formally became a partner in the project, and the orbiting platform became known as the International Space Station (ISS). NASA scientists and engineers learned a lot from their Russian counterparts about space stations.

The ISS was built over a period of 12 years. It is made up of a series of pressurized modules, structural parts, and large solar panels. Russia rocketed the first segment of the space station into space on November 20, 1998. Some of the modules were launched into space and then docked with the existing space station structure. Others were delivered directly to the orbiting space lab by US space shuttles.

AN ENGINEERING MARVEL

A marvel of engineering, architecture, technology, and international cooperation, the ISS weighs nearly 1 million pounds (454,000 kg).[1] It spans the size of a football field and orbits Earth every 90 minutes at an altitude of 248 miles (400 km).[2] The first three-member ISS crew arrived on November 2, 2000, and the ISS has been continuously occupied ever since.

GETTING TO THE ISS

A Soyuz spacecraft delivered the first crew to the ISS in late 2000. The space shuttle carried them home in March 2001. The shuttle went on missions back and forth to the ISS between 2001 and 2011. Astronauts and cosmonauts traveled on both the space shuttle and the Soyuz to the ISS. When the shuttle was retired in 2011, Soyuz became the only spacecraft capable of taking people to the orbiting laboratory. Today, NASA astronauts travel aboard Soyuz capsules to reach the ISS. Unpiloted Russian Progress spacecraft and European Automated Transfer Vehicles (ATV) carry supplies to the station. A Soyuz spacecraft always stays at the space station to act as a lifeboat in case there is an emergency and the ISS must be evacuated.

ISS crews are made up of six members who live on and work at the space station for six months at a time. The experiments done at the ISS are designed to help with future space exploration as well as life on Earth. Agricultural experiments aboard the space station are carried out to learn how plants grow in space. Growing plants in space may be necessary to help sustain human life during long stays on the moon and Mars. Studies of the moon and the rest of the solar system are conducted at the ISS. Scientists aboard the ISS can also observe weather patterns on Earth.

Experiments at the space station may also hold the key to curing serious diseases. Medical researchers send experiments into space to be carried out by astronauts. In order to study the proteins that make the body function disease-free, they grow crystals of these proteins to observe them. On Earth, gravity flattens and distorts these crystals, but in space they develop into large shapes, perfect for

The ISS underwent enormous growth between 1998, *left*, and 2011, *right*.

study leading to the development of drugs to combat these illnesses.

The space station is history's largest spacecraft. It requires maintenance and repairs on a regular basis, both inside and out, while it is in orbit. This is the same kind of work that will have to be done on spacecraft during long-term flights to Mars and destinations even farther away. Information gathered from keeping the space station operational, replacing parts, and doing general mechanical upkeep will reduce risks on future missions to distant planets.

An ISS module known as the Cupola features large windows that give astronauts incredible views of Earth.

Robotic spacecraft can explore areas far beyond the reach of human explorers.

CHAPTER 9

WHERE NO ONE HAS GONE BEFORE

R obotic spaceflights are less expensive and less risky than piloted ones. Over the last 50 years, probes have rocketed to every planet in the solar system. They have also visited comets and asteroids. These mechanical explorers have relayed a wealth of information back to Earth and continue to do so. The United States and Russia have historically been the most active when it comes to launching probes, but in recent years other nations, including China and Japan, have sent robotic spacecraft into the solar system.

Many advocates of piloted spaceflight believe sending people into space is a critical part of space exploration. But it is clear robotic explorers have an important part to play. The track record of incredible missions in the early 2000s demonstrates the worth of robotic probes to space exploration.

MISSIONS TO THE OUTER SOLAR SYSTEM

The *Voyager* spacecraft flew past Saturn, but the *Cassini-Huygens* probe was planned to stay. It entered orbit around Saturn on July 1, 2004. Launched in 1997, the *Cassini* spacecraft and its *Huygens* lander was a joint project of NASA and the European Space Agency (ESA). It sent back stunning photos of the ringed planet after entering orbit. On December 25, 2004, *Huygens* separated from *Cassini* and headed for Titan, Saturn's largest moon. It landed successfully and transmitted data to Earth. *Huygens* stopped sending data soon after, but *Cassini* remains in operation today.

The *New Horizons* mission is estimated to cost approximately $700 million.

The dwarf planet Pluto is one of the least understood bodies in the solar system. It is so far from Earth that even the most powerful telescopes show it as a tiny speck in the sky. NASA's *New Horizons* probe is designed to change this. Launched on January 19, 2006, *New Horizons* is traveling more than 620,000 miles (1,000,000 km) per day.[1] It is expected to reach Pluto in July 2015. The nine-year trip will give humans the first close look at the dwarf planet.

Other nations are becoming active in space as well. China sent its *Chang'e 1* and *2* probes to the moon in 2007 and 2010. China hopes to establish a robotic base on the moon by 2020. *Chandrayaan-1* became India's first lunar probe in 2008. The Japan Aerospace Exploration Agency (JAXA) sent an orbiter, *Akatsuki,* to Venus in 2010. The year also marked the return of JAXA's *Hayabusa* spacecraft, launched in 2003. *Hayabusa* traveled to an asteroid, collected samples from its surface, and returned to Earth.

FUEL OF THE FUTURE

Japan's *Hayabusa* spacecraft used an innovative type of engine. Rather than a liquid engine, as with the Apollo CSM, or a solid engine, as with the shuttle SRBs, it used an ion engine. This engine type uses electricity and xenon gas to shoot tiny particles out of the spacecraft at high speed. The acceleration of ion engines is much, much lower than with other engine types. More powerful stages using liquid or solid fuels must be used to put the spacecraft into space before the ion engines can be used. But once in space, an ion engine can run for months at a time, building up speed slowly.

TO MARS

Mars has long attracted the interest of space explorers. Even before spaceflight was invented, it captivated science fiction writers. In 1898, H. G. Wells wrote his classic, *War of the Worlds,* a fictional account of Martians attacking Earth. Radio, television, and movies later presented their own accounts of fictional Martian mayhem.

In reality, scientists have been working for decades to determine whether life has ever existed on Mars. The United States has been the most successful nation when it comes to sending probes to Mars and gathering information and photographs. NASA's series of rovers in the 1990s and 2000s achieved incredible results. The *Sojourner* rover landed aboard the *Pathfinder* spacecraft in July 1997. *Sojourner* is 24.5 inches (63 cm) long and 10.9 inches (28 cm) tall.[2] NASA sent twin rovers, *Spirit* and *Opportunity*, in January 2004. They contain more sophisticated instruments and are each 5.2 feet (1.6 m) long and 4.9 feet (1.5 m) tall.[3] Incredibly, *Opportunity* continued to function in 2013, far beyond its expected 90-day mission. In 2012, NASA landed the most advanced rover yet. *Curiosity* is the size of a small car.

On many of these missions to Mars, scientists have been trying to determine if water was ever present on the

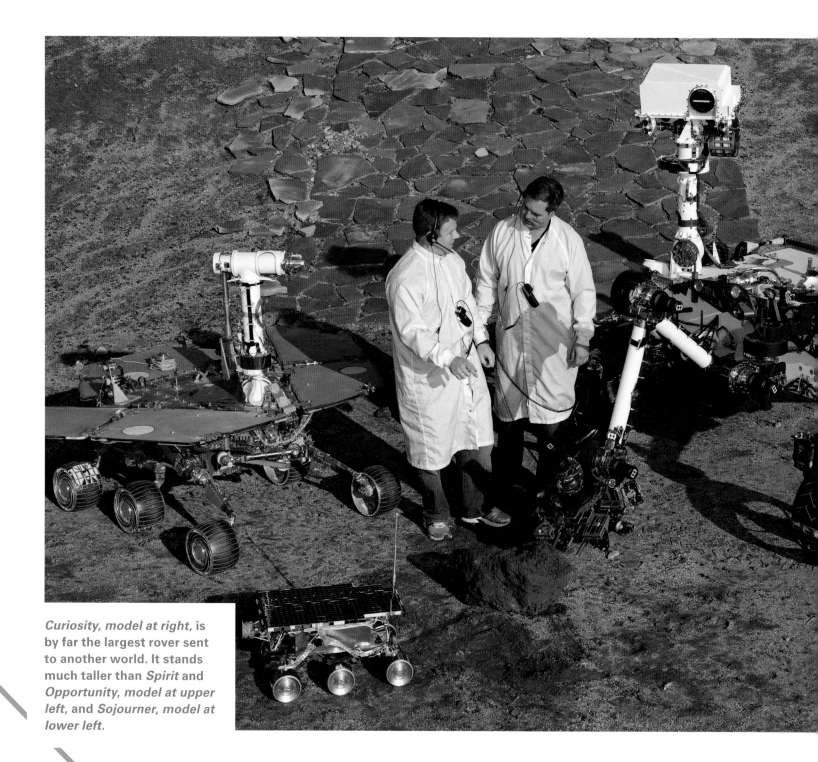

Curiosity, model at right, is by far the largest rover sent to another world. It stands much taller than *Spirit* and *Opportunity,* model at upper left, and *Sojourner,* model at lower left.

planet. Since scientists know water is essential to sustain life, proof water once existed on Mars may mean life was there as well. Both *Spirit* and *Opportunity* found clues water once existed on the planet. *Opportunity* found the greatest evidence yet in June 2013 with the discovery of clay-rich rock on Mars. That finding led scientists to believe water probably existed on ancient Mars billions of years ago and conditions there might have supported life.

In 2013, the United States planned for a piloted Mars mission in the 2030s. Trips to Mars will start with orbits of the planet, similar to those astronauts made around the moon in the 1960s. Landings on the planet will follow. However, tremendous technical hurdles will need to be overcome. Radiation in space is dangerous to astronauts, and during such a long trip they would receive an unhealthy dose of it. If a medical emergency or ship failure occurred, rescue would be impossible with the spacecraft so far away. Communication is also a challenge. NASA experienced slight radio delays during the Apollo program, since the radio waves took slightly more than one second to travel the distance between Earth and the moon. But Mars is so far away signals take several minutes to travel each way, making instant communication impossible.

Because of these challenges, NASA intends to complete several missions as stepping-stones to a piloted Mars landing. A return to the moon and a new mission to an asteroid by 2025 are two of the planned steps. To accomplish this, NASA is overseeing the development of a new spacecraft, the first since the retirement of the shuttle. Called the Orion Multi-Purpose Crew Vehicle (MPCV), the spacecraft is a throwback to the old capsule-shaped modules of the Apollo era. However, it is capable of holding more astronauts, up to six. It is also packed with the latest computer technology, far beyond the primitive computers used during the Apollo program. A new launch vehicle, the space launch system (SLS), recycles parts from the space

Artist concepts show the SLS looking like a cross between the Saturn V and the space shuttle.

shuttles, including SSMEs and SRBs. It is expected to be even more powerful than the Saturn V.

PUSHING FORWARD

Other nations also plan to return to the moon and push forward to Mars. In October 2003, China became the third nation to launch a human being into space when Yang Liwei orbited Earth aboard *Shenzhou 5*. Two years later, *Shenzhou 6* carried two Chinese crew members into orbit. A piloted mission with a space walk followed in 2008. China put a small space station, *Tiangong 1*, into orbit in September 2011. Subsequent missions have docked with the station. The China National Space Administration plans to continue piloted spaceflights, including some to the moon and eventually Mars. Though Russia, the United States, and the European Union continue to cooperate in space, China has pursued its own program. At the same time, private companies across the world are beginning to take steps into space in search of profit.

The next generation of robotic probes and space telescopes is currently in development. They promise to

Yang Liwei completed 14 orbits aboard *Shenzhou 5*.

provide unprecedented information about the universe. The James Webb Space Telescope (JWST) is among the most ambitious projects. The successor to the HST features a 21-foot (6.5 m) mirror that sees in the infrared region of the spectrum rather than in the visible region.[4] Viewing in infrared can reveal objects hidden to a visible-light telescope. In 2013, the JWST was slated to launch in 2018.

INCREDIBLE EXPLORATIONS

Space is the newest frontier for human exploration. For centuries people have studied the lands, seas, and skies of Earth. But it was not until technology made it possible that humanity stepped into space. Beginning with a tiny metal sphere in 1957, the advances made in space exploration have opened the universe to us. Only a few years later, people flew to space to see it with their own

COMMERCIAL SPACE

Private corporations are now beginning to carry out space missions for a profit. One of those companies, SpaceX, has already started launching its unpiloted *Dragon* spacecraft atop its Falcon 9 rockets to bring supplies to the ISS. NASA has given SpaceX a 1.6-billion-dollar–contract for the unpiloted supply flights.[5] Eventually, the company plans to fly people into space aboard *Dragon* spacecraft. Long-term plans include missions to Mars.

eyes. Not long after that, astronauts stood on the surface of the moon.

Though outer space is an expansive area to explore, it is still important for humanity to take care of this latest frontier. Decades of launching satellites and other spacecraft has left Earth's orbit cluttered with debris. These materials, which can be hazardous to other spacecraft, are known as space junk.

Piloted explorations of space provided some of the most dramatic moments in human history. At the same time, robotic explorers were dispatched to every corner of the solar system. Without the need for things like air and food, these probes studied planets, moons, and asteroids for years at a time. They sent back tremendous amounts of information and photographs, revealing for the first time the appearance of the outer solar system.

Inventing the technology and tools for space exploration led to many discoveries about the nature of our universe. But it also resulted in dramatic changes to our everyday life on Earth. Advances in cameras, clothing, food, and medicine

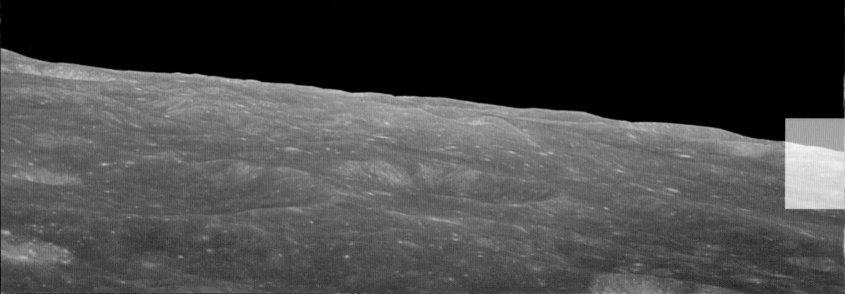

came from space programs. Commonplace devices such as smartphones can trace their roots back to technologies developed for space exploration.

Astrophysicist Neil DeGrasse Tyson has been a passionate advocate of continued space exploration. He believes space is like any other frontier, and that the human spirit of exploration and discovery spurs us to explore it:

> *Ever since there have been people, there have been explorers, looking in places where others hadn't been before. Not everyone does it, but we are part of a species where some members of the species do—to the benefit of us all.*[6]

The recognition of our own planet's tiny place in the universe compels many to continue exploring space.

TIMELINE

1957 The Soviet Union launches *Sputnik 1,* the first satellite to orbit Earth, on October 4.

1958 The United States launches its first satellite, *Explorer 1,* on January 31; the National Aeronautics and Space Administration (NASA) begins operations on October 1.

1959 *Luna 2,* a Soviet probe, crash-lands on the moon on September 14, becoming the first object made on Earth to reach the moon.

1961 Yuri Gagarin of the Soviet Union becomes the first human in space on April 12. Alan Shepard becomes the first US astronaut in space on May 5.

1962 John Glenn becomes the first American to orbit Earth on February 20.

1963 Valentina Tereshkova becomes the first woman to go into space in June.

1965 Cosmonaut Alexei Leonov becomes the first person to walk in space on March 18.

1966 Sergei Korolev, the leader of the Soviet space program, dies suddenly on January 14; *Gemini 8* succeeds in docking with a target vehicle—the first docking in space—on March 16.

1967 Three astronauts are killed when a fire breaks out during a run-through on the launchpad on January 27; cosmonaut Vladimir Komarov dies when *Soyuz 1* crash-lands during reentry in April.

1968 *Apollo 8* becomes the first piloted spacecraft to orbit the moon in December.

1969 Apollo 11 astronauts Neil Armstrong and Edwin "Buzz" Aldrin land on the moon on July 20.

1975 US and Soviet spacecraft dock in space on July 17 as part of the Apollo-Soyuz Test Project, the first joint space venture between the two countries.

1981 The first US space shuttle, *Columbia,* is launched on April 12.

1986 The space shuttle *Challenger* explodes shortly after takeoff, killing everyone onboard on January 28.

1998 The first segment of the International Space Station is launched on November 20.

2003 The space shuttle *Columbia* disintegrates upon reentry, killing the entire seven-member crew on February 1.

2011 *Atlantis* launches on the final US space shuttle mission on July 8.

ESSENTIAL FACTS ABOUT SPACE EXPLORATION

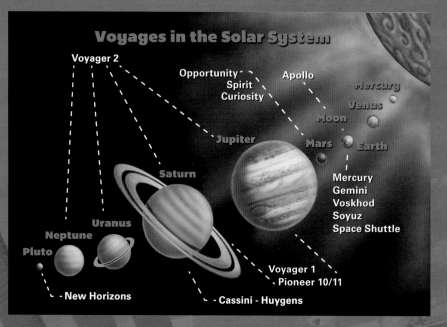

Voyages in the Solar System

Voyager 2

Opportunity
Spirit
Curiosity

Apollo

Mercury

Venus

Moon

Jupiter

Mars

Earth

Mercury
Gemini
Voshod
Soyuz
Space Shuttle

Saturn

Uranus

Neptune

Pluto

- New Horizons

Voyager 1
Pioneer 10/11

- Cassini - Huygens

KEY DISCOVERIES AND THEIR IMPACTS

On April 12, 1961, Yuri Gagarin becomes the first person to orbit Earth aboard *Vostok 1*, proving human beings can survive in space.

On July 20, 1969, Neil Armstrong and Edwin "Buzz" Aldrin walk on the surface of the moon, demonstrating that complex missions involving rendezvous, docking, and EVAs are feasible.

In 1989, *Voyager 2* completes a 12-year planetary Grand Tour, flying by Jupiter, Saturn, Uranus, and Neptune. The probe sends back the first close-up photos of Uranus and Neptune.

KEY PLAYERS

Konstantin Tsiolkovsky developed early theories on rocketry and space travel.

Robert Goddard built early liquid-fueled rockets.

Wernher von Braun developed the Saturn V rocket.

Sergei Korolev led the Soviet Union's space program.

Yuri Gagarin was the first person in space.

Neil Armstrong was the first person to walk on the moon.

KEY TOOLS & TECHNOLOGIES

Multistage rockets made it possible to launch satellites and spacecraft out of Earth's atmosphere.

Space suits allowed astronauts and cosmonauts to float freely outside of their spacecraft and walk on the lunar surface.

Rendezvous and docking made complex missions possible, including those in the Apollo program.

Space stations gave astronauts and scientists places to carry out long-term experiments in space.

QUOTE

"That's one small step for a man, one giant leap for mankind."

—*Neil Armstrong*

GLOSSARY

aeronautical
Relating to the science of flight.

artificial satellite
A manufactured object or vehicle that orbits a planet.

docking
Having two spacecraft connect in outer space.

flight simulator
A machine that allows the user to experience what it is like to pilot an aircraft.

gravitational pull
The force of attraction that bodies exert on each other due to their masses.

meganewton
The metric unit for force. One meganewton equals the amount of force needed to accelerate 1 million kilograms by 1 meter per second squared.

probe
A robotic spacecraft equipped with instruments and sensors, often used to explore outer space.

propulsion

The force that moves something forward, such as a rocket.

rendezvous

The meeting of two spacecraft in orbit, accomplished by maneuvering with rocket engines.

suborbital

A flight that does not orbit Earth.

thrust

The force propelling a rocket.

warhead

The section of a missile that holds the explosive charge.

ADDITIONAL RESOURCES

SELECTED BIBLIOGRAPHY

Cadbury, Deborah. *Space Race: The Epic Battle Between America and the Soviet Union for Dominion of Space.* New York: HarperCollins, 2006. Print.

Oberg, James. *Star-Crossed Orbits: Inside the US-Russian Space Alliance.* New York: McGraw-Hill, 2002. Print.

Wiens, Roger. *Red Rover: Inside the Story of Robotic Space Exploration from Genesis to the Mars Rover Curiosity.* New York: Basic, 2013. Print.

FURTHER READINGS

Bizony, Piers. *The Space Shuttle: Celebrating Thirty Years of NASA's First Space Plane.* Minneapolis: Zenith, 2011. Print.

Chaikin, Andrew, and Alan Bean, with Victoria Kohl. *Mission Control, This Is Apollo: The Story of the First Voyages to the Moon.* New York: Viking, 2009. Print.

Launius, Roger D. *Space Stations: Space Camps to the Stars.* Washington, DC: Smithsonian, 2003. Print.

WEB SITES

To learn more about exploring space, visit ABDO Publishing Company online at **www.abdopublishing.com**. Web sites about exploring space are featured on our Book Links page. These links are routinely monitored and updated to provide the most current information available.

FOR MORE INFORMATION

For more information on this subject, contact or visit the following organizations:

Kennedy Space Center
State Road 405 East
Kennedy Space Center, Florida 32899
866-737-5235
http://kennedyspacecenter.com
This launch site has been used for every NASA human spaceflight since 1968. Visitors can tour the launch areas, meet veteran astronauts, see actual rockets, and train in space simulators.

Smithsonian National Air and Space Museum
Independence Avenue at Sixth Street, SW
Washington, DC 20560
202-633-2214
http://airandspace.si.edu
The National Air and Space Museum has the largest collection of historic aircraft and spacecraft in the world. The Apollo 11 command module, *Columbia*, is in the museum's main building in Washington, DC.

SOURCE NOTES

CHAPTER 1. SPACE-AGE WONDERS

1. Carl Sagan. *Pale Blue Dot*. New York: Ballantine, 1997. Print. 6.

CHAPTER 2. BLASTOFF!

1. William J. Jorden. "Soviet Fires Earth Satellite into Space." *On This Day*. New York Times, 5 Oct. 1957. Web. 12 Sept. 2013.

2. Ibid.

3. "V-2 Missile." *Encyclopaedia Britannica*. Encyclopaedia Britannica, 2013. Web. 12 Sept. 2013.

4. John Noble Wilford. "With Fear and Wonder in its Wake, Sputnik Lifted Us into the Future." *New York Times*. New York Times, 25 Sept. 2007. Web. 16 Sept. 2013.

5. "Vanguard." *Encyclopaedia Britannica*. Encyclopaedia Britannica, 2013. Web. 12 Sept. 2013.

6. "Sputnik 2." *National Space Science Data Center*. NASA, 16 Aug. 2013. Web. 12 Sept. 2013.

CHAPTER 3. EARLY SPACE EXPLORERS

1. "Astronaut Selection and Training." *NASA*. NASA, 2011. Web. 12 Sept. 2013.

2. Deborah Cadbury. *Space Race: The Epic Battle Between America and the Soviet Union for Dominion of Space*. New York: HarperCollins, 2006. Print. 200.

3. "Luna 2." *National Space Science Data Center*. NASA, 16 Aug. 2013. Web. 12 Sept. 2013.

4. "Escape Velocity of Earth." *Department of Physics*. University of Urbana-Champaign, 19 July 2006. Web. 12 Sept. 2013.

5. "Freedom 7 MR-3." *Mercury*. Kennedy Space Center, 5 Apr. 2002. Web. 12 Sept. 2013.

6. Jay Barbree. *"Live from Cape Canaveral": Covering the Space Race from Sputnik to Today*. New York: HarperCollins, 2007. Print. 57.

CHAPTER 4. A NATIONAL PRIORITY

1. John F. Kennedy. "John F. Kennedy Moon Speech." *NASA*. NASA, 12 Sept. 1962. Web. 16 Sept. 2013.

2. John F. Kennedy. "Address by President John F. Kennedy to the UN General Assembly." *US Department of State*. US Department of State, 20 Sept. 1963. Web. 12 Sept. 2013.

3. "Mariner 2." *National Space Science Data Center*. NASA, 16 Aug. 2013. Web. 12 Sept. 2013.

4. Amy Shira Teitel. "The Soviets' First 'Space Rendezvous.'" *Discovery News*. Discovery, 17 Aug. 2012. Web. 12 Sept. 2013.

5. Alexei Leonov. "The Nightmare of Voskhod 2." *Air and Space Magazine*. Smithsonian, Jan. 2005. Web. 12 Sept. 2013.

CHAPTER 5. TESTING LIMITS

1. Mary C. White. "Detailed Biographies of Apollo 1 Crew – Ed White." *NASA History*. NASA, 4 Aug. 2006. Web. 12 Sept. 2013.

2. Ibid.

3. "Gemini 6A." *NASA*. NASA, 13 Mar. 2003. Web. 12 Sept. 2013.

4. J. Terry White. "Emergency in Space." *American Aerospace*. Seattlepi.com, 14 Mar. 2011. Web. 12 Sept. 2013.

5. Larry Merritt. "The Abbreviated Flight of Gemini 8." *Boeing*. Boeing, March 2006. Web. 12 Sept. 2013.

SOURCE NOTES CONTINUED

CHAPTER 6. TO THE MOON

1. "Apollo 1's Tale Retold: 'Fire in the Cockpit!'" *NBC News*. NBC News, 27 Jan. 2007. Web. 12 Sept. 2013.

2. Deborah Cadbury. *Space Race: The Epic Battle Between America and the Soviet Union for Dominion of Space*. New York: HarperCollins, 2006. Print. 305.

3. Karl Tate. "NASA's Mighty Saturn V Moon Rocket Explained." *Space.com*. Space.com, 9 Nov. 2012. Web. 12 Sept. 2013.

4. Ibid.

5. "One Giant Leap For Mankind." *NASA*. NASA, 19 July 2013. Web. 12 Sept. 2013.

6. Ned Potter. "Neil Armstrong: How 'One Small Step' Became First Words on Moon." *ABC News*. ABC News, 2 Jan. 2013. Web. 12 Sept. 2013.

7. "Neil A. Armstrong Biography." *Glenn Research Center*. NASA, Aug. 2012. Web. 12 Sept. 2013.

CHAPTER 7. AFTER THE RACE

1. "Lunar Roving Vehicle." *Apollo Program*. Smithsonian National Air and Space Museum, n.d. Web. 12 Sept. 2013.

2. "NASA Mars Orbiter Images May Show 1971 Soviet Lander." *NASA*. NASA, 11 Apr. 2013. Web. 12 Sept. 2013.

3. "Venus." *Encyclopaedia Britannica*. Encyclopaedia Britannica, 2013. Web. 12 Sept. 2013.

4. "Hubble Space Telescope." *NASA*. NASA, 29 Apr. 2010. Web. 12 Sept. 2013.

5. "Challenger Disaster." *History Channel*. History Channel, 2013. Web. 12 Sept. 2013.

6. Tariq Malik. "NASA's Space Shuttle by the Numbers: 30 Years of a Spaceflight Icon." *Space.com*. Space.com, 21 July 2011. Web. 12 Sept. 2013.

CHAPTER 8. ORBITING SCIENCE LABS

1. "Facts and Figures." *International Space Station*. NASA, 28 July 2013. Web. 12 Sept. 2013.

2. "Higher Altitude Improves Station's Fuel Economy." *International Space Station*. NASA, 14 Feb. 2011. Web. 12 Sept. 2013.

CHAPTER 9. WHERE NO ONE HAS GONE BEFORE

1. "Mission FAQs." *New Horizons*. NASA, 12 Sept. 2013. Web. 12 Sept. 2013.

2. "Rover Sojourner." *NASA*. NASA, 8 July 1997. Web. 12 Sept. 2013.

3. "Mars Exploration Rover." *NASA*. NASA, 2004. Web. 12 Sept. 2013.

4. "About the Webb." *The James Webb Space Telescope*. NASA, n.d. Web. 12 Sept. 2013.

5. "COTS 2 Mission Press Kit." *NASA*. NASA, 2012. Web. 12 Sept. 2013.

6. "Space Exploration Quotes." *Neil DeGrasse Tyson*. Neil DeGrasse Tyson, 2013. Web. 12 Sept. 2013.

INDEX

ABOUT THE AUTHOR

Robert Grayson is an award-winning former daily newspaper reporter and the author of books for young adults. Throughout his journalism career, Grayson has written stories on historic events, sports figures, arts and entertainment, business, and pets. These stories have appeared in national and regional publications, including *New York Yankees* magazine and *NBA Hoop*. He has written books about the Industrial Revolution, animals in the military, and animal performers, as well as the environment, law enforcement, and professional sports.